Basis for [...]
In the Far [...]

By NATHANIEL [...]

America is in a world war. That it came into that war by way of the Pacific and the Far East is, says Nathaniel Peffer, the logic of history. We have been marching toward that war since 1900, possibly since 1840. In short, Pearl Harbor was not cause; it was effect. By common consent, the Pacific and Far East, now and in the future, is America's first sphere of activity.

That being so, for America there are now only two choices: either to prevent future wars in that part of the world or to fight in them. Which shall it be? Can we prevent future wars in the Far East? If so, how? Can we find a basis for enduring peace in the Far East? If so, what is it? This is only another way of asking: Why and for what is America fighting?

Mr. Peffer believes that given victory in the war and foresight in the making of the peace, we can save ourselves from a fate in the Far East such as hung over Europe for centuries. But to achieve this end two things are imperative: Japan must be crushed and evicted from the continent of Asia. And China must be helped to develop industrially until she is as strong and independent as America. In a strong China, Mr. Peffer proves, lies the hope of economic stability not only for Japan and the rest of Asia, but for Europe and America.

Succinct, compelling, discerning, this informed discussion of the problems involved in winning both the war and the peace is one of the most important books written for Americans for many years. It is published in cooperation with the International Secretariat, Institute of Pacific Relations.

No. 5165

BASIS FOR PEACE IN THE FAR EAST

Published in co-operation with the International Secretariat, Institute of Pacific Relations. Small parts of this book are adapted from a monograph prepared by the author for the Institute of Pacific Relations under the title Prerequisites to Peace in the Far East. *The author alone, however, is responsible for statements of fact and opinion.*

Basis for Peace in the Far East

By

NATHANIEL PEFFER

New York and London

HARPER & BROTHERS

PUBLISHERS

Table of Contents

BASIS FOR PEACE IN THE FAR EAST

Chapter One

The Future in the East

AMERICA IS AT WAR, ENGAGED IN A WORLD WAR
for the second time in a generation. Between
this war and the war twenty-five years earlier
there are two salient points of difference, however. Then American troops were fighting mainly
on a single sector in France. Today they are
fighting on all the seven seas and all the continents. Then America had some option; it entered the war by its own decision, freely arrived
at according to its lights. Now it is in the war
because it was attacked and some three thousand
men were killed on its own soil within a few
hours. America was still engaged in internal debate about what course it should take in the
European war when the bombs fell on Pearl
Harbor and Japan declared war, to be followed
in a few days by Germany and Italy. For
America the governing fact about this war is

I

that it was drawn into it not by way of Europe, where it had done all or nearly all it could to bring about the defeat of one of the antagonists, but by way of the Far East. And the governing fact about America's role in world politics is that this was in the logic of American history. Pearl Harbor was not an accident or a coincidence. It was not a cause of conflict, but an effect of conflict.

We are at war the world over because of events lying in Eastern Asia. It is not easy to imagine oneself explaining to the re-embodied spirit of Washington or Jefferson or Hamilton how and why the destiny of the republic they wrought may be determined on the Yangtsze or the Irrawaddy or the Ganges, seven or eight or nine thousand miles from the Atlantic seaboard on which they brought a nation into being; but it is so. Whatever may be said about our ability to be any more faithful to the original injunction against entanglement in Europe's wars than we have been in the past, it can be said with certainty that we shall not be able to keep out of future wars in Asia, if there are to be more wars in Asia. By so much America's place in history is complicated,

2

its future path made more precarious. Three times in the history of the American republic there have been major European wars: the Napoleonic wars, the war of 1914, the war of 1939. Each time there has been a conscious resolve to keep out, each time America has failed to keep out. Whether it was drawn in by circumstances beyond its control or because it could not and did not want to remain indifferent to the disposal of power in Europe and the moral values involved, is a matter of historical speculation and beyond possibility of demonstration. The fact is that in all of Europe's major wars since the beginning of American history America has been a participant. This is not the point at which to argue whether it can break the consistency of the record in the future or must either commit itself to organized efforts to prevent wars in Europe or be resigned to fighting in them. But in the Far East America is already committed. Not by accident did Japan direct its first blows at America when it decided to challenge the Occident. Not by accident has America taken over the major responsibility for the conduct of the war in the Pacific and Far East. By common

3

consent, America's included, that is America's first sphere of activity. In that quarter of the world certainly we can resign ourselves to the necessity of choice: either prevent future wars or fight in them, no matter how many of them there may be and how devastating.

The object of this book is to ask which it shall be. Can we prevent future wars in the Far East? If so, how? Is there a basis for enduring peace in the Far East? If so, what is it? This is another way of asking: what is America fighting for in the Far East? What do we hope to gain by war in that part of the world? What kind of peace will be deemed worth the sacrifice of life and wealth which will be exacted of us before we have victory? For America certainly it is not enough to occupy ourselves with plans for international reconstruction focusing on Europe. For us there is neither security nor emancipation from recurrent war unless a tenable basis for peace can be laid in the Far East too. We stand now at crucial decision in that part of the world. We can delude ourselves no longer in the belief that the Far East is remote, exotic, and dissociated from the concerns that touch us vitally. It has been brought

4

permanently into the world political system. Japan's adhesion to the Axis and the declaration of war on America by Germany and Italy immediately after Japan opened hostilities against America and Great Britain were symptomatic. The Far East now is as Europe was four hundred years ago. Either a basis for lasting peace must be found for that part of the world now or it must go the way of Europe, chained to a wheel of periodic bloodletting, of chronic warfare, generation on generation, time without end. And that will touch America directly, even more directly than the European blood feud. America will be to the Far East as England has been to the European continent—unwilling to be drawn in, unable to keep out, caught in its fateful pull. As we look on Europe's mournful history now, we can see its tragic making. As we look at the last thirty years in particular, we can tell ourselves: we might have known. We see, too late, the mistakes, of omission rather than commission. The retrospect in Europe is clear. The prospect for the Far East can be projected with equal clarity, if there are the same errors of omission. The larger circumstances are analogous, the forces are compounded of the same elements. By the way in which the present war in the Far East is settled, by the kind of peace that is made, it will be determined whether a generation from now we shall have to say of that part of the world, too: we might have known. In that case the words will have a tragic connotation for America. For American boys will be plighted to death in battle in distant parts, generation on generation, time without end.

What, then, are we fighting for? Assuming that we win, what terms of peace shall we dictate, what kind of system shall we establish in the Far East?

For the Far East the problem is fortunately easier than for Europe. It is less fraught with intangibles and with complexities. One may well despair of the problem of establishing peace in Europe. The European problem is almost four-dimensional, almost beyond reach. The politics of Europe is so deeply enmeshed in intellectual, emotional, almost spiritual fixities, so deeply embedded in the past, that it seems almost hopeless to try to bring order out of the chaos that has been solidified, as it were, by tradition. Who can

6

draw a map of Europe that will not leave embittered minorities in one country or another, minorities of blood and language and religion and culture? How organize the continent as a rational economic unit without dispossessing vested interests in one area or another? How give it political unity, a community of thought and feeling and aspiration and values, when hate has for so long bred hate, injustice for so long bred injustice, and the feudist's oath is almost given with the mother's milk? We may succeed, and certainly we must try, if we mean to save Western civilization; but if we do succeed we shall have brought off one of the most difficult political feats in man's history.

It is entirely otherwise in the Far East. There the political problem is not complicated by any long heritage of hatred or memory of ancient wrongs. There is no deep encrustation as the result of the shifting permutations of high politics. The vested economic interests are not long established and do not carry with them survival for one national group or another. There are few or no intangibles, few or no subtleties. In contrast with Europe, the political problem is

7

one-dimensional. The cause of wars can be isolated, so that it is visible and can be attacked. Once that cause is laid, there is as good a prospect of lasting peace as mankind can hope for in its present estate. Given victory in the war and foresight in the making of the peace, we can absolve ourselves from a fate in the Far East such as has hung over Europe for centuries. This is or should be the principal aim of America in the war. It should be America's main task in the formulation of the peace. What is involved in it is the subject of this book.

Chapter Two

The Making of a War

BEFORE AMERICA CAN PLAN ITS COURSE IN THE making of the peace and its place in world politics thereafter, it must get clearly in mind how and why it got into the Second World War. Pearl Harbor, it has been said, was an effect, not a cause. But an effect of what? What were its antecedents?

In general, the history of wars shows that they cannot be explained by the events that immediately precede them. The status of Danzig was only the pretext for the present war in Europe, the occasion for its start. The conflict had been set in motion years before—perhaps with the Spanish civil war, perhaps with the Italian invasion of Ethiopia, perhaps with the advent of Hitler to power in Germany, perhaps with the Japanese conquest of Manchuria, perhaps even with the signing of the Treaty of Versailles. In

9

the same way the assassination of the Austrian Archduke Franz Ferdinand was only the occasion for the start of the First World War. The course of the conflict had been set years before, perhaps as early as the turn of the century, with the beginning of the Anglo-German naval race. In a sense the same reasoning holds for Pearl Harbor. It was only the occasion for the Japanese-American war. But in the main the prelude to the war in the Pacific is unique in that it contains within itself the whole explanation for the war. It was inclusive as well as climactic. It revealed with clarity and finality the fundamental cause of the war and, more particularly, why America became a participant.

The last phase of the crisis in the Pacific was played out between July 23 and December 7, 1941. It began with the announcement on July 23 of a so-called agreement between Japan and the Vichy regime whereby Japan and France were "to co-operate in military matters for the defense of French Indo-China," as the protocol signed a few days later euphemistically put it. Even before the formal signature Japan had begun the occupation of southern Indo-China. With Indo-China occupied, Japan was at the borders of Thailand and could invade that helpless land at will. Then Japan would be at the borders of Malaya, from which it could open an attack against Singapore. If the attack were successful, the British Empire would be severed, the southern Dominions would be all but cut off and Great Britain itself deprived of sources of essential supplies. By so much Germany's victory in Europe would be made more likely and in the event of German victory the United States would be for all practical purposes in a state of siege, lying between two victorious, aggressive, fascist empires. The danger was plain and the United States retaliated at once. On July 25, two days after announcement of the Japan-Vichy agreement, the American government decreed the freezing of all Japanese credits in this country. It was followed at once by Great Britain, the British Dominions, and the Netherlands East Indies.

The effect was to establish a world-wide economic blockade around Japan and thus to put Japan under sentence of eventual economic strangulation. For without access to at least some part of the world for raw materials Japan certainly cannot fight and probably cannot live or at least cannot maintain its industrial structure. Japan was placed in a dilemma. It had either to fight or to wait for slow emasculation unless it could by chance get around the dilemma by bringing about a compromise with the United States. It sought to do the latter. While there had been sporadic diplomatic conversations between the Japanese and American governments in the previous weeks Japan now asked for formal negotiations toward a general settlement of Japanese-American controversies in the Far East. Prince Konoye, the Japanese prime minister, in August proposed a personal meeting between himself and President Roosevelt to that end. Then followed three months of protracted negotiations moving steadily toward impasse. But before formal acknowledgment of deadlock both sides declared themselves finally and beyond misapprehension. Each put its minimum terms for an agreement, thus precluding the historian's usual task of deducing later from incomplete and prejudiced evidence the causes for a war.

Early in the negotiations the Japanese had stipulated that they be permitted to station troops

permanently at various points in China. To this
the United States objected in a formal note of
October 2. It is to be observed that the negotiations had already broadened out beyond the subject that had precipitated them, which was the
Japanese occupation of southern Indo-China and
the retaliatory freezing of Japanese credits. Then
on November 20 Japan made another offer. It
agreed to withdraw from southern Indo-China
if the United States would lift the ban on the sale
of oil; on China it was noncommittal. The United
States on November 26 countered with its final
terms. It laid down certain general principles:
respect for the territorial integrity of all nations,
noninterference in the internal affairs of other
countries, equality of commercial opportunity,
etc. Then it laid down certain definite stipulations,
the most important of which was that Japan
withdraw completely not only from Indo-China
but from China proper. There were ten days of
silence, and then Japan answered with the
bombers over Pearl Harbor. But one hour after
the attack began, a documentary reply was made,
too. It consisted mainly of bitter recriminations,

most of which turned on America's insistence on the evacuation of China.

In other words: what presumably brought on the last phase of the crisis and the prelude to war was the Japanese occupation of southern Indo-China and the freezing of Japanese credits. But Japan offered to withdraw from southern Indo-China in exchange for the relaxation of the freezing order, which meant returning to the situation before July 23. The real occasion for the crisis, then, could be settled. What could not be settled, what constituted the real stumbling block, was the status of China, which ostensibly had nothing to do with the final controversy. The United States insisted that Japan abandon its design for conquest of China; Japan refused. On all else there might be compromise; on this there could be no compromise. The issue could no longer be evaded. One side or the other had to retreat. Japan had to abandon the aim of its four-year war against China, the aim of thirty or more years' imperial ambition on the Asiatic mainland, or America had to submit to Japanese control over China. Neither side would retreat. There was war. But the war was over China, and not over any of the collateral effects of the European war such as the Japanese encroachments on the colonies of European countries defeated by Germany.

Over China, then, the Second World War spread to the Pacific and the Far East. Perhaps it is better to say that a world war for mastery of Europe combined with a world war for mastery of China. In either case it was the fulfillment of the logic of world politics that there should have been a war over China and, furthermore, that America should be engaged in it. Into the making of that war went all the forces of nineteenth-century politics; all the policies of the Great Powers contributed to that end. It was the time of the great Western irruption the world over. It was the time when the industrial revolution had given to the major countries of the West instruments of conquest that we now see at their highest efficacy in the bombing of Europe and given them, as well, need for conquest. The quest for raw materials, though the object was profitable industrial production rather than successful warfare, was one driving force. The search for outlet for the commodities produced in unprece-

15

dented volume was another. Every storehouse of
natural resources in the world had to be taken
over for exploitation, every land with enough
inhabitants to constitute a profitable market ap-
propriated as a market. Nationalism and the
exaggerated pride of national place, the dominant
spirit of the time, acted as goad. The forces arising out of the industrial revolution and nationalism combined to form the propulsive drive that
we know as imperialism, and imperialism in effect
was the overrunning of the whole world and the
subjection of weak peoples everywhere.

China was not excepted. On the contrary, it
was the highest prize of imperialistic conquest—
India having already been absorbed by the British
Empire. And for a hundred years before 1941,
from 1842 when the British battered down the
doors of China, there had been a progressive
reduction of China—a competitive reduction,
each Great Power vying with every other for
primacy. Their combined efforts were enough to
reduce China to a state of semidependency: parts
of its territory sheared off by one Power or another; strategically situated ports allocated as
settlements and concessions and governed by

foreign Powers; the country divided into foreign
spheres of influence; foreign garrisons posted at
various points and foreign fighting ships plying
its inland waters; its public services under foreign supervision or control; its economy so
ordered that the first rewards went to the foreigner. But China never was completely conquered. It remained intact on the delicate balance
of international rivalries. No one Power dared to
make an overt attempt at outright and exclusive
conquest, for that would have united the other
Powers against it. Nor could they agree on
partition, for there was too much jealousy among
them, too much distrust, and moreover the
European balance of power was becoming too
precarious. The year 1914 was not too far off.
The inconclusive rivalry was China's good for-
tune but the Occident's tragedy, as present events
testify. For it was laying a train of conflict and
moving it forward relentlessly. As tension arose
the world over, as the prelude to 1914 was being
enacted, the joustings for China became more
active. They came to formal war only once—that
between Russia and Japan in 1904. But war was
latent always. There was the kind of conflict that

must resolve in war unless it is allayed in time. The conflict was over the fate of China. The issue was—and still is—was China to remain an independent nation or become a colony of some great empire, and, if the latter, a colony of what empire?

The issue remained unresolved because it was cut across by the World War of 1914. Thereby it was simplified. By reason of the war there came about that which had not obtained before, thus letting China survive. One Power got a free hand. That Power was Japan. The war gave Japan opportunity and immunity. All other rivals were preoccupied in a struggle for survival. It was the First World War that made Japan a World Power: politically because it could embark with impunity on a career of aggrandizement, economically because not only did it obtain a virtual monopoly on the market of Eastern Asia but because the demand of the warring countries for manufactured materials gave an impetus to Japanese industrialization. Japan had manifested desires for aggrandizement before. It had begun, indeed, soon after it had emerged from seclusion in 1854. It formally joined the other aspirants

18

for hegemony over China in 1894 with its quick and decisive victory over the Chinese. But it was only a secondary contender, still overshadowed by the might of aggressive European Powers.

After 1914, Japan had less need for caution. It became a primary contender, and therewith a new chapter opened in the Far East. Beginning immediately on the outbreak of the war in Europe with the occupation of the German territorial holdings on the north coast of China and following a few months later with the Twenty-One Demands, which would have made China a Japanese protectorate, Japan started on that which it is now attempting to carry to conclusion —the conquest and absorption of China. From that purpose it has never since deviated. There were temporary pauses and variations in tempo, imposed by external developments, but the direction never changed. Sometimes, as on the occasion of the Twenty-One Demands, there was overt action, sometimes the oblique approach, as when by loans and subsidies to certain Chinese groups between 1917 and 1919 an attempt was made to install puppet regimes in China. But the movement was direct from 1915 to the seizure of Man-

19

churia in 1931, the semidetachment of North China between 1935 and 1937, and the invasion of China itself in 1937. The time of decision was nearing in the Far East. For the first time a formal, unmistakable effort was under way to appropriate China as a colony. By all the logic of the past it was destined to bring about a general war. In 1941 it did.

Two external developments served to impose variations in tempo on Japan but at the same time to set it firmer in its course and to foreshorten the end. The first was the unexpectedly early conclusion of the war in 1918, which left the United States with unprecedented military power. Japan had to be circumspect. When the Washington Conference was convened in 1921 on American initiative Japan was held to an accounting and, with American naval might still in the ascendant, Japan beat a retreat. But the issue in the Far East was becoming clarified. To the Japanese at least it became clear where lay the source of the most formidable obstacle to their designs for imperial grandeur. The logical conclusion they drew from their perception gave form to all their subsequent policies and acts. It led straight to Pearl Harbor.

20

The second external development was the spread of nationalism throughout the nonwhite world, particularly in those areas that had been denied nationhood by virtue of subjection to one empire or another. The idea of nationalism had already taken root in such areas before the World War, having been transmitted from its Occidental place of origin because facility of communication cannot be restricted to commodities alone. Consciously or unconsciously, we exported our concepts along with cigarettes, textiles, implements, and gadgets. And nationalism was one of the dominant concepts of the Western world in the nineteenth century, the other being democracy. The idea of nationalism had taken root before the war. The war gave it rapid growth, principally by reason of the body of Wilsonian doctrines. The Western world may have remained unresponsive to the appeal of such doctrines as making the world safe for democracy, the rights of small nations, self-determination, and justice to the weak; but they found welcome lodgment in the minds of the peoples deprived of the benefits innate in those doctrines. There was an upsurge of nationalism in every part of the world and the ensuing years were marked by successive colonial revolts. Such revolts and the attempts to suppress them were the stuff of international politics in the period immediately following the war.

Of no part of the world was this more conspicuously true than of China. There had been a nascent nationalism in China since the revolution of 1911 that overthrew the alien Manchu dynasty. It was forced to maturity after 1918 by two rebuffs. The first was at the Versailles Peace Conference. China formally petitioned for some measures toward restitution of sovereignty. Its appeal was ignored. Worse than that, in the peace settlement itself the parts of China that had been a German leasehold were awarded to Japan instead of being restored to China, although China had been in the war as an ally of the victors. The second rebuff was at the Washington Conference, where China again asked for restoration of sovereignty and, though not ignored, was put off with amiable but meaningless generalities. Two international conferences had been held with the avowed purpose of laying the foundations of durable peace, one of them concerned with the Far East alone. And China remained a semi-

22

dependent country, with foreign outposts on its soil, outposts that might serve as bases for further advance whenever any empire chose. Inversely, the Great Powers were left in a position of rivalry for ascendancy in China, the rivalry that had caused enough concern to warrant the summoning of the Washington Conference and that quite properly was recognized as a threat to peace in the future. The danger of war had been recognized and the cause of war left untouched. Indeed, it may be said that the last chance to prevent a general war in the Far East was at the Washington Conference.

In China the effect was explosive. It was as if something long pent up were finding outlet. Waves of feeling swept the country—nationalist, anti-imperialist, antiforeign. A deep internal change was coming over the country. It was accelerated and intensified by intervention from an external source—Russia. Russia's motives still cannot be disentangled. In part, there was the Lenin thesis that the capitalist empires could be undermined only by striking at their imperialistic foundations. Thus, colonial rebellions should be fostered. China offered the most promising field, since the Chinese were already embittered and China was one of the strongholds of British imperialism. In part, there was also no doubt Russia's historic rivalry with Great Britain for primacy in Asia and its historic quest for a warm-water port. It must be remembered that Russia had been driving relentlessly across Northeastern Asia toward Manchuria and the China coast before being stopped by Japan. Whatever the reason, Russia—under the guise of the Communist International—made an agreement with the Chinese Kuomintang or Nationalist Party and sent military and civil advisers. With the assistance of the communist technique of organization and propaganda the Nationalists swept over the country, galvanizing the people with the cry, "Down with Imperialism." And Western imperialism was being undone. The Western Powers beat a retreat. With singular lack of foresight they neither made concessions voluntarily nor offered resistance. For the former there was no excuse; for the latter there was the logical explanation that their people were too war-weary for colonial expeditions on the other side of the globe. With every foreign retreat the Chinese

24

advanced more boldly, demanded more and took more. In five years the foreign position was all but undermined, and China felt strong enough even to break with Russia. For the latter there were a number of reasons, perhaps the main one being that the communists were overreaching themselves and the Chinese began to fear that they might be supplanting one foreign master by another.

The Chinese continued on their own momentum, and it became clear then that any empire that wanted to maintain its rights in China would have to fight for them. The Western empires were not inclined to fight, and probably could not have fought. But the Japanese also had rights in China—in Manchuria, particularly. And they were not exhausted by four years of war and they would obey their rulers. The Chinese made manifest their intention to reclaim sovereignty in Manchuria too. Japan saw the risk. It had no inclination to make concessions, but it was prepared to resist. The forces of collision were moving. In 1931, Japan struck in Manchuria, and the rest is recent history. The Japanese military machine was under way. The hour of decision had arrived in the Far East. China was to be a colony—a Japanese colony—unless force was interposed to obstruct Japan, force interposed by China or by some Western country or both. No check could come from Europe, since Europe was already in the prelude of the Second World War. America was still in its isolationist phase and, moreover, was concerned with Europe. Once again Europe's blood feud gave Japan a free hand. If check was to come, it had to come from China itself. China girded itself for the struggle for selfpreservation. Formal war awaited only the incident to precipitate it. The incident came in the summer of 1937, and the war began that is still in progress and that was eventually to draw in America and amalgamate with the European war for world mastery.

This, then, was the making of the war in the Far East, and plainly into it went all that was most authentically of the time. The attempt to conquer China itself was part of the larger expansive movement of the nineteenth century, a movement that derived its force from the industrialization of production in the West. The rivalry for domination in China was integral to

26

a time when nationalism was the principle of order and the reward of national expansion was economic gain as well as glory. The emergence of Japan into competition with Western empires also was inherent in the scheme of the time, for easier communications made for the transmission both of ideas and technical knowledge, thus endowing Japan with nationalism, the capacity to produce cheaply by machinery, and the motives for expansion arising from both. It was delusive folly to have expected that industrialization and the instruments of power that it yielded could be confined to Western nations. By the same process nationalism was transmitted to China and, as a result, the resolve to regain independence, by force if necessary. The Russian intervention in support of China was part of the social struggle on the issue of the principle of economic organization. The failure of the Western empires to make concessions to the aspirations of the Chinese, which might have warded off the climax, derives from the spirit of imperialism, which is incompatible with concession, and from the conditions of the postwar period, when relaxation of control of colonies entailed the risk of immediate loss, which the Western countries could not bear. The failure to do the opposite, namely, crush Chinese intransigence at the start, was inevitable, given the postwar psychological reaction and postwar weakness. Out of these came China's full challenge to independence, a challenge that carried a threat to Japan's imperial pretensions. Japan, being an empire in the ascendant, could and would brook no threat to its pretensions, especially at a time when Europe's new embroilment again gave it opportunity, an opportunity that might not recur. This, too, was part of recent history. Thus step by step, moving apparently with a kind of fatality but actually only with the spirit of the age, the Far East was carried forward to war and catastrophe. The war is the expression of a century, the logical conclusion and climax of a century.

Chapter Three

America and the Far East

THE WAR IN THE FAR EAST CAME ON THE ISSUE of China's status as a nation and was the fulfillment of the logic of history. But why did it involve America? Why America as the main protagonist of one side of the issue? Why America, dedicated from its founding to the principle of nonentanglement in external politics and the wars of other nations? Why should it be American flyers who are being shot out of the air over the mountain passes in Yunnan Province? By what perverse mischance or irrational calculation or personal heedlessness was America brought to risk national existence on the fate of a country six thousand miles from its center of population, of wholly alien blood and culture and tradition and background? This, too, must be understood if we are to deal intelligently with the questions raised in the peace settlement or with the one

29

question that matters vitally to America: how can it be brought about that this shall not be again?

It can be understood only against the realization that in this, too, there has been logical progression. As the Far East has moved stage by stage to war for reasons inherent in the forces at work in that part of the world, so America has moved stage by stage to war in the Far East for reasons inherent in the forces at work within itself and in its relations with that part of the world. The fact has been easily perceptible in the last ten years, could have been discerned in the preceding ten years, and has been latent for the larger part of America's history. The causes are less clear and still cannot be established beyond challenge. It is in truth almost inexplicable that a people coming from Europe to the eastern shore of a fresh and uninhabited continent three thousand miles broad should find themselves in a few generations committed in the lives of their sons and their fortunes to the affairs of a country four thousand miles from the western shore of that continent, after consciously having resolved throughout their history to cut themselves off from the affairs of the continent from which they sprang. Even before Washington delivered his famous injunction, the founders of the republic almost without exception had laid down as a guiding principle for the new nation abstention from European affairs. Emancipation from European politics was, indeed, one of the impelling motives for the establishment of an independent nation. For Europe meant perpetual war, and concern with the politics of Europe meant plighting the nation to perpetual war. From Europe, then, the American people declared themselves apart, though to Europeans they were racially akin and from Europe they derived their institutions, culture, mores, fundamental ideas, and attitude toward life. The resolve may have been violated, but it was never waived. It has been one of the nation's deepest convictions. Yet with Asia, with which there was and could be no community of any kind, not the most tenuous link, there has been conscious, direct, willed concern. With Europe, no entanglement; with Asia, active participation in all its remote, exotic politics. Why the contrast?

Many reasons enter, as in all complex political situations. No doubt there has long been in this

31

country a certain feeling of sympathy for the Chinese people, but this is probably not so much the cause of a political attitude as the effect of one. It is true, as is commonly said, that the large body of missionaries periodically returning from China have created a public opinion favorable to the Chinese; but missionaries have returned from other countries without the same result in American opinion. There have been numerous American missionaries to Japan too. No doubt, the convictions, prejudices, and vagaries of certain individual American officials have played some part. The usual citations in this connection are Theodore Roosevelt, Henry Cabot Lodge, John Hay, Admiral Mahan, and others of the group mainly responsible for the taking of the Philippines in 1899, thus giving the United States a territorial outpost in the Pacific and a political commitment. The Boy Scout ebullience of that group can be conceded, but their historical importance in American-Asiatic relations is open to doubt. To establish their importance in the sense that they are responsible for America's direction in the Far East, it would be necessary to show that there had never been any such inclination before and that if they had never lived there would have been no such inclination. Yet there is ample internal evidence that there had been marked interest in the Far East long before their time and that at the end of the nineteenth century the interest was mounting in circles far wider than theirs. They themselves were effect as much as cause. Finally, allowance must be made for the weight of bureaucratic habit and the influence of what is called national prestige. Governments often have policies because they have had them. To change them is to make confession of previous error, and thus to do self-inflicted injury to one's amour propre as individual and prestige as a nation. Neither individuals nor nations are given to inflicting such injuries on themselves. Furthermore, each successive secretary of state, for example, is unconsciously indoctrinated by the cumulative practices of his predecessors or by the permanent staff which initiates him into the mystery of the diplomatic craft and state secrets. He gives evidence of initiation, of "belonging," by adopting the principles and practices of those who have gone before. If such have been the nation's policies, they must be his policies. Thus

33

he shows his place in a distinguished lineage. To an extent, therefore, the United States has taken a position in the Far East because it had taken that position before.

These are contributory reasons but contributory only. They might explain a transient national attitude but not a strong undeviating stand in the politics of power, with all the attendant risks of war. Any country in any geographical or political setting has had more substantial grounds for what it conceives to be the national interest, if that conception is consistently maintained. And this must be emphasized: in no other single policy, no declaration of aim, no national pursuit of a political end, has the United States been more undeviating than in its Far Eastern policy. Not even the Monroe Doctrine is to be excepted.

In the critical months before Pearl Harbor, when the United States and Japan marched straight to conflict, there was nothing essentially new. All that went into that controversy was present in embryo almost a hundred years before —when Japan was still a hermit island kingdom, incidentally. What America did or tried to do in those months was a projection of what it was

34

starting to do a hundred years before. The position that brought it into conflict with Japan over China was one on which it had taken its stand a hundred years ago, however unconscious then of possible future consequences. In other words, the roots of American participation in conflict in the Far East lie deep in American history. Hoover and Stimson, Roosevelt and Hull, have only carried to logical if fateful conclusion what was set in motion by their predecessors.

It is tempting but unwise to draw too sharp a contrast between America in Europe and America in Asia. It is true that America forswore any part in European politics, but it never renounced economic relations with Europe. Very specifically the proscription was always of alliances and meddling in intra-European concerns. It was believed—and in the early days rightly—that it was possible to have economic dealings with Europe without any political entanglements. Isolation, in other words, was only political nonparticipation, not nonintercourse. No such distinctions could arise with reference to the Far East, partly because the idea that there could be political complications seemed remote and mainly because there was not the heritage of a fear of wars, as in Europe. In the Far East we had in mind economic relations, at first passing over the thought of political complications and later accepting them as preferable to renouncing economic relations. In short, America has never believed in isolation in any real sense. With reference to Europe it has believed in political isolation only, with reference to Asia in neither political nor economic isolation. In the American attitude to the two continents there is a contrast, but it should not be pushed too far; as far as it holds, however, it is revealing.

The Far East has exercised a strong pull on the United States almost from the beginning of American history. Historical mysticism is always dubious, but there is something almost beyond the rational in the way the American people have been drawn ever westward, even since before they were securely established on the Eastern shore of the continent. There are material explanations, of course, for what was called manifest destiny: free land, better land, the opportunity for which even the original immigrants had left Europe and that seemed to beckon ever further. But the continent curiously did not set the bounds to manifest destiny. The other shore of the Pacific was as alluring as the West and the Western Coast of the continent. There was trade with China almost from the beginning; the first trading ship sailed for Canton in 1785. The Far East was not of another world to the New England merchant ship owner and exporter or the Western fur trader. It was distinctly in the economic consciousness of the time. The United States has been an active competitor for the trade of the Far East, of China especially, since there has been Far Eastern trade. Through the first half of the nineteenth century it was Great Britain's principal competitor in that area and second to Great Britain, already mistress of the seas and first in the world's trade.

By the middle of the century the American clipper ships were unequaled on the seas. The Pacific was an accepted area of American enterprise, accepted by Americans as within their rights—long, long before Theodore Roosevelt and Henry Cabot Lodge, it will be observed. With a kind of historical unity, it was at Hawaii that the issue in the Pacific was first drawn by and for

America. What happened in the 1840's with respect to Hawaii (then called the Sandwich Islands) was a foreshadowing and a symbol. As Hoover and Stimson, Roosevelt and Hull, in the last ten years, so Tyler and Webster, Fillmore and Webster a hundred years earlier. The extension of European power and influence having already begun, both England and France were casting covetous glances at Hawaii. There were all the moves preliminary to absorption. The United States vetoed, in strong and unmistakable terms. Through the decade of the 1840's it was issuing warnings that any attempt to establish the sovereignty of any European Power over Hawaii would be regarded as an unfriendly act. This, it should be observed, while half of the North American continent was still wilderness and the frontier was not far beyond the Mississippi. Finally, after a formal advance in Hawaii by France in 1849, the United States sought to forestall further efforts by recognizing the independence of Hawaii, thus officially adopting the role of opposition. It was then that President Fillmore, informing Congress of the reasons for his action and summarizing the point of view of three successive American administrations, made a historic statement of America's role in the Pacific. In recognizing the independence of the Hawaiian Islands, the American government was influenced, he said, "by the consideration that they lie in the course of the great trade which must at no distant day be carried on between the Western coast of North America and Eastern Asia. . . . I need not say that the importance of these considerations has been greatly influenced by the sudden and vast development which the interests of the United States have attained in California and Oregon, and the policy heretofore adopted in regard to those islands will be steadily pursued."

Thus, it was not Hawaii in itself that mattered but Hawaii as the stepping stone to Eastern Asia, and in Eastern Asia what mattered was the "great trade" that North America would someday have there. And this, it should be marked, when there were no more than a handful of Americans on the West Coast and the land west of Kansas and Nebraska was practically uninhabited. But Fillmore's words were prophetic. They stated a profound and lasting truth of

39

America's relations with the outer world, and in the light of 1941 it was fitting that they should have been evoked by the islands in which Pearl Harbor lay.

Fillmore was not adumbrating in a void or indulging in premature pseudo-geopolitical mysticism. He was recapitulating, carrying to logical conclusion, what had been said and done by his predecessors. They and he were drawing direct inferences from a clear and practical situation. Not only had the trade of the Far East had a material appeal but just in those years the Far East was calling for attention. It was in 1842 that China had been forced open to foreign trade by Great Britain. So far from unconscious of the political and economic implications was the United States that immediately thereupon President Tyler sent Caleb Cushing as American commissioner to establish formal relations with China. The conception of the relations desired was manifested when Cushing pressed for and obtained China's consent to a most-favored-nation clause in the first treaty signed by the two countries. By this provision any concession or benefit granted by China to any other country was automatically extended to the United States. This was not wholly new or unthought of by Americans interested in the Far East, as is indicated by the fact that an American naval officer at Canton, Commodore Kearny, had already suggested to Chinese officials at that port that such privileges be given to American traders. At any rate, most-favored-nation treatment was asked for and obtained. And there in germ was American policy in the Far East: equality of opportunity, of economic opportunity in particular. Come what may in that part of the world, there must be no impairing of American trading rights, of America's position as a competitor on equal terms with any other trading nation. Whatever may happen politically, China must remain a free field for American trade. In other words, China's trade must not be sequestered as a monopoly by any other Power, however strong in a military sense. In short, the Open Door policy, the policy America has with increasing vigor sponsored since the end of the nineteenth century, that on which in the last analysis America and Japan came to collision in 1941.

It was England that forced China open but

America that forced Japan open. That fact must be borne in mind in weighing any theory that America has become involved in the Far East out of sudden vagary or caprice. America was an active contender for position and perquisites in the Far East as soon as the Far East was brought into relations with the West. From the beginning America was reserving its rights and staking out its claim, though a claim different in kind from the avowedly imperialist Powers. In 1851, less than ten years after the opening of China and seven years after the conclusion of the first Chinese-American treaty, it was decided, again by the Fillmore administration, to send an expedition to Japan to establish political and economic relations. Mainly, America was prompted by the general interest in the Far East, accentuated by events in China; in addition, there was the unwillingness to be forestalled by England, as in China. Again it must be pointed out that America was England's closest competitor in Far Eastern waters. When Commodore Perry sailed in 1852 the instructions he bore with him as commander of the expedition read:

"Recent events—the navigation of the ocean

42

by steam, the acquisition and rapid settlement by this country of a vast territory on the Pacific, the discovery of gold in that region, the rapid communication established across the Isthmus which separates the two oceans—have practically brought the countries of the east in closer proximity to our own; although the consequences of these events have scarcely begun to be felt, the intercourse between them has already greatly increased and no limits can be assigned to its future extension."

It was the same general theme that was expressed in the explanation for the policy of obstructing the conquest of Hawaii by European Powers.

There was another indication, perhaps even more revealing. In this period, too, there began the agitation for the building of a transcontinental railroad. It spread rapidly and won wide support. State legislatures, chambers of commerce, public men, and disinterested advocates of internal development, as well as promoters and speculators, took part. There were petitions and memorials to Congress, pamphlets widely circulated, hearings of congressional committees and speeches in both Houses. One note ran through the whole discussion: the advantage of such a railroad in giving easier access to Eastern Asia. Legislatures of numerous states then and now notoriously isolationist with respect to Europe sent memorials to Congress urging the necessity of giving the whole continent a shorter route to the Far East. The trade of the East, fabled throughout the ages, was the high reward of enterprise, and it could and would be America's. The American continent opened on the Pacific. Connect the whole continent with its Pacific shore and it would command the trade of the East. It was as if the principal purpose of a transcontinental railroad were Far Eastern trade and the development of America itself were incidental. And it is significant of the state of opinion in the country that the most active proponents of the railroad, as well as the lobbyists, chose as their strongest talking point the prospect of Eastern trade. The Far East may have seemed remote to the next generation of Americans but not then. In the middle period it was a part of the world which was active and pressing in the American consciousness.

44

In the next generation there was in truth a recession in American activity in the Far East. This is what has given rise to the misconception that America's interest in that part of the world is of recent making and therefore episodic. In fact, the inactivity between the 1850's and the end of the century was a deceptive interlude. It was the exception in American history rather than the rule. The explanation of the interlude is simple: the Civil War, the Reconstruction, and the great period of internal development, with the building of railroads, the tapping of new sources of raw materials, and the organization of the key industries. In America as elsewhere this was the period when the industrial revolution was coming to maturity and yielding its highest rewards. There was neither time nor energy for external economic activities, nor was there need. Foreign trade and foreign investments exercised little appeal when there were bonanzas to be opened at home. America, in short, was exclusively engaged in domestic exploitation.

Out of the same set of reasons came the end of the interlude in the 1890's. The bonanzas were all staked out. The railroads were built. Free land

45

was gone. Raw material sources had come or were coming under control. Furthermore, the United States was no longer an exporter of raw materials only. It was beginning to export manufactured products. It was entering an area of trade in which it did not have the virtual monopoly of certain primary products, but would have to compete for markets. The curve of economic progress was still to rise, but it was beginning to flatten. While the country was far from economic saturation point, the stage had come when high rewards were no longer to come so easily and carry the same rate of profit. The automobile age and its high promise could not yet be envisaged. What seemed clear on all the perceptible evidence was that for the brightest prospects America would have to look outward. And the fact that this was the time when the other industrialized countries were carving out great economic empires all over the world did not contribute to introversion here. America turned its gaze outward too. It was not out of caprice or accident or individual idiosyncrasies that just then it took its first steps outside the continental limits of the republic. And it was consistent with the country's past that its scrutiny should have turned westward and that the first steps were beyond its Pacific shores in the direction of Asia.

Appropriately Hawaii was the first object of attention. American influence there had been growing steadily and by the latter part of the century Hawaii had become a kind of unofficial protectorate. Early in the 1890's, for a combination of reasons that need not detain us, since they were occasion rather than cause, there began a movement for annexation to the United States. As might be expected, the movement was initiated and led by Americans. It failed, because Grover Cleveland, then president, was revolted by the patent chicanery of the whole affair. The failure was only temporary. In 1898 came the war with Spain. That war, it will be remembered, was caused presumably by Spanish oppression in Cuba, an island in the Caribbean, in Atlantic waters. It ended with the annexation of Hawaii, in the mid-Pacific, and the taking of the Philippines, islands at the other end of the Pacific, some nine thousand miles from Cuba. The debate over the taking of the Philippines was revealing. As is well known, the Spanish war was not

47

popular with influential groups in industry and finance. They were outspoken in their opposition. This was as long as only Cuba and the Caribbean were involved. There was a sudden and marked change with the naval victory of Manila Bay and the occupation of Manila. Business, which had been lukewarm, became enthusiastic. The reason was made plain by the almost unanimous advocacy of retaining the Philippines, and the main reason for retaining the Philippines, was, as in the case of Hawaii fifty years earlier, not the Philippines in themselves but as a gateway to the markets of the Far East. Economic journals glowed with descriptions of the prospects of that market, the fabulous wealth of the East that would be funneled through the Philippines. Though more restrained than in the memorials urging the transcontinental railroad fifty years earlier, the note was the same. The result, too, was the same. The debate in Congress and the press on whether to keep the Philippines was intense; the dangers of imperialism were eloquently pointed out. But the Philippines were kept. For the first time the American flag was planted on soil far from the Western Hemisphere; the country became in-

volved in the power politics of distant areas, the
peculiarly dangerous politics of colonial rivalry,
and hostages were given in the Far East. But it
is a fallacy to say, as sometimes is said, that the
country became involved in the Far East because
it took the Philippines; on the contrary, it took
the Philippines because it was involved in the Far
East. The Philippines was an effect, not a cause.

The connection between the Philippines and the
larger Far Eastern stake was unmistakably re-
vealed when almost simultaneously the United
States intervened directly in what appeared to be
a climax in the struggle for ascendancy in China.
In 1898 there had begun the preliminaries to what
seemed the certain partitioning of China among
Great Britain, Germany, France, and Russia.
Each was marking off its sphere. In 1899 the
United States sent to all the Powers its famous
Open Door notes. They sought to pledge each
Power not to put into effect in its sphere in China
any taxes, charges, or other regulations which
would discriminate against other countries. Again
America was reserving its rights as historically
stated. For this was repetition in enlargement of
the stand taken by America in China in the

49

1840's. Whatever might be the fate of China, whether broken up or not into several spheres, colonies, or other fragments, America would have equality of economic opportunity in any part of China, no matter what Great Power was in control there.

It was the American injunction in the Pacific, never waived, never modified. America would have no part in the struggle for China directly. It wanted and would take no Chinese territory for itself; it had had chances to do so and refused. It would not seek to restrain others from taking territory in China. But if they did, it would not suffer thereby any diminution of its opportunity for trade. It would insist on equality of opportunity, a fair share of the Chinese market in unrestricted competition. And when shortly after 1899 it became apparent that if China were partitioned there would and could be no Open Door, since monopoly was one of the purposes of acquisition of Chinese territory, America restated and expanded its position in another series of notes. It sought pledges from all the Powers for the preservation of the integrity of China. And on this America has stood ever since: The Open

Door in China and the integrity of China—the
integrity of China, as thereby and thereby alone
could America be assured of the Open Door and
unimpeded access to the Chinese market. From
this it may at times have wavered, but never
departed. It may at times have seemed to retreat,
but the retreat was only temporary. At the most,
its movement was two steps backward and three
steps forward, advancing as the crisis in the Far
East advanced. To that extent and in its peculiar
way it was involved in the Far Eastern conflict,
involved in the imperialistic conflict in the Far
East. It was involved not as contender for spoils
but as leveler of injunctions against such imperialistic spoliation as militated against its rights and
interests. The role was negative from the point
of view of the conventional struggles of imperialism, but positive in the effect on American relations. It was a commitment no less for being a
commitment by veto.

In the opening years of the twentieth century
the main threat to China's integrity came from
Russia, and against Russia America directed all
its protests and its political and diplomatic opposition. To Japan, however, fell the obligation of

51

taking up Russia's challenge, for Russian success would have vitally imperiled Japan. And it is noteworthy, as well as revealing, that in the war between Japan and Russia that broke out in 1904 America was wholeheartedly pro-Japanese in public opinion, in financial support, in moral support. It was through Theodore Roosevelt's mediation that Japan obtained a better peace than it could have obtained by its own military efforts, for it was nearing the point of exhaustion. Japan won and supplanted Russia not only in the Chinese territory that Russia had occupied but in Russia's political ambition. As has been said, it started at once an advance in the direction of dominion over China. At once, too, the pro-Japanese feeling in America ended, and there began the friction between the countries that has been steadily exacerbated ever since. In proportion as Japan advanced, American opposition increased. And as European influence in the Far East diminished because of Europe's war America was left alone as the spearhead of opposition. Indeed, from the Japanese point of view it can be said justly that the obstruction to the realization of its ambitions has come from

America mainly if not exclusively. It was America that warned against the execution of the Twenty-One Demands and thus stiffened China. It was America that called Japan to accounting at the Washington Conference and compelled Japan to disgorge most of its gains of the preceding years, both in China and in Siberia. It was America that heartened the Chinese to withstand Japanese penetration both financially and politically. It was America that took the van in the effort, though unsuccessful, to prevent the Japanese from completing the conquest of Manchuria after 1931. It was America that at the end stood in the way of Japan's consolidating its military victories in the war with China after 1937. Even Russia, with which Japan has had recurrent difficulties, made a nonaggression pact with Japan and stood aside.

The issue in the Far East had narrowed down to America versus Japan, because the sole remaining threat to China's integrity came from Japan. And it was a threat that carried the negation of America's ends in the Far East more conclusively than any that had gone before. For the so-called New Order in the Far East proclaimed

53

by the Japanese after their occupation of a large part of China had as its first principle the establishment of an economic monopoly in China. Thus America arrayed itself squarely and uncompromisingly against Japan. Thus it would have arrayed itself squarely and uncompromisingly against any other country having the same ends. Thus it will presumably array itself in the future against any country that should supplant Japan in striving for the same ends. The issue will be the same: the integrity of China as a condition of equality of opportunity for America in China. It is the issue on which America has advanced toward war through a large part of its history, the issue on which it has become involved in the most terrible war in its history. Therefore Pearl Harbor; therefore at Pearl Harbor Japan struck first at America when it elected to plunge into the Second World War. For America was its foremost enemy.

Chapter Four

The Principles of the Peace Settlement

SUCH HAS BEEN THE MAKING OF THE WAR IN which America has staked the lives of its young men and its future as a nation. To what end, then, is it fighting? Assuming victory (only on that assumption will America have any freedom of decision), what kind of peace do we want in the Far East and what are the terms that will assure such a peace?

The answer to the question follows by direct logic from the analysis of that which caused the situation to arise. What caused the war has been seen. The peace will come by eliminating that cause. One world war has had to be fought because it could not be determined by peaceful means whether China should be independent or a colony and, if a colony, belong to what empire. Other world wars will have to be fought until that question is settled once and for all. If, then, the primary object is a system of relations in the Far East under which peace can be maintained and America in particular emancipated from the fate of periodic wars on the Asiatic continent, what concretely must be the main provisions of the treaty of peace?

First, as a necessary preliminary, Japan must be not only defeated but crushed—maimed and left helpless, beyond possibility of recovery for a long period. It must be driven from the Asiatic continent and from the islands off the continent and in the Pacific. It must be returned to the geographical position it occupied when it emerged from seclusion.

Second, China must be made completely independent. Its territory must be cleared of all foreign troops; all foreign settlements and concessions must be retroceded; all foreign privileges in infringement of its sovereignty must be canceled. The relation of other Powers to China must henceforth be exclusively that of one country trading with another.

Third, such economic arrangements must be made in the Far East as will assure to Japan livelihood on a standard common to modern industrial peoples. This means that no artificial obstructions must be interposed against its access to raw materials and markets in Asia on equal terms with any other country. Implicit in this is the forfeiture by the Western Powers of the economic priority they have always assumed to be theirs in the Far East.

Fourth, there must be a fundamental change in the position of those parts of Eastern Asia that have hitherto been colonies of Western empires. This does not necessarily require complete evacuation or grant of full independence in all instances, but it does require, as a minimum, material concessions in the form of greater native autonomy and systematic preparation for independence, with withdrawal by the empires in stages.

Fifth, China must be not only restored to full independence but strengthened. This can most effectively be done by way of large-scale economic assistance to enable it to industrialize as rapidly as possible. Thereby a double purpose will be served. China will have the physical means to safeguard its independence, thus preventing the renewal of competitive encroachment by other Powers, that which brought about the present

57

war. This is the indispensable condition to the maintenance of peace in the Far East. Further, through the industrialization of China the Western nations can escape the worst consequences of the readjustment to a peace economy, perhaps can escape the extremities of the economic crisis that lies ahead for the Western world.

The net general effect of this program, it will be seen, is retreat by the West. The West must abandon the pretensions which have sustained it in power, glory, and profit in the last hundred years. It must renounce world mastery in the sense that it has exercised mastery since the early nineteenth century, if not before. It must give up rule in the Far East politically. It must give up all hope that the riches of the East will be forever funneled off into European and American capitals, that the trade of the East will forever be an exclusive perquisite of the West. It must do so if there is not to be chronic war for the prizes of the East. It must do so because it really has no choice. For the age of imperialism is done and the day of Western domination of the world must be committed to the dead past. This is history's decree, not our option. History will set the pattern of the East-West relationship because the forces in modern history have laid down the lines of movement.

This is coming to be recognized as an abstraction. Its concrete application in political and economic relations and the political and economic consequences of its application are not yet recognized. In the larger sense we shall not be free agents in the Far East, come what may in the present war. And that was foreshadowed long before the war. It could have been foreseen as soon as the ferment of nationalism began stirring in the East. And on the day that Japan invaded China in 1937 it was ordained with finality that the West must lose priority in the Far East. And thus it is now, beyond peradventure of doubt, whatever the form of the events that betide there. If the Japanese win, the outright eviction of the West follows as a matter of course. That is one of Japan's major purposes in resorting to war, and it gave conclusive evidence of intent by what followed its victories in the Philippines, Netherlands East Indies, and Burma. If China is victorious—that is, if China escapes subjugation to the Japanese by virtue of its own efforts and the help of the United Nations—the West will be evicted from the Far East, too. In either case the West will be forced out.

It must be remembered that the train of events leading to the climax in the Far East was set in motion by the advent of Chinese nationalism and the resolve to emancipate the country. It was this that led to collision with Japan. And China will not have borne the sacrifices laid on it by years of invasion just to return to its old subordinate position. It will not have lost millions of dead and suffered devastation of the land and then meekly submit to Western control of its largest cities. If it has succeeded in repelling the gravest menace to its national existence, made by the strongest of those who aspired to conquest, it will not accept semisubjection to those less strong. China will be conscious of its powers and assert them. And the defeats and humiliations suffered by the once ruling nations of the West will not have endowed the white empires with any derived moral authority. That which was known as the white man's prestige, something apart from and beyond his intrinsic power, has passed. The glow of invincibility is no longer about the white empires.

They will no longer exercise authority by assertion or by symbol. They will hold only such position as they can prove their capacity to hold. In either case the West will be forced out of the Far East. But the manner in which that is effected and the purposes for which it is effected will be so different according to whether China or Japan wins, that while the fact is the same, the results will be incomparable.

If the West is evicted from the Far East by virtue of a Chinese victory, it will suffer a loss only measured against its past position and aspirations. The Western Powers will lose territorial outposts and special privileges. These, however, were originally taken and later held as tokens against each other, as pawns in an imperialistic game, with all China as the stake. If all the Powers are dispossessed at once they will be at no disadvantage relative to each other. They will be at disadvantage relative to China only in that they will have to renounce perforce any opportunity to control China, but in compensation therefor they will be absolved of the obligation to maneuver to forestall each other with all the weapons of power politics, to arm against each other with death-dealing weapons, to live in constant danger of war for imperial prizes, regardless of whether the prizes are intrinsically worth the cost of armament and war. On balance they will gain more than they lose. Economically, they will be at no disadvantage relative to each other. They will deal with China as equals—equal with respect to each other and with respect to China.

Mainly, if deprived of territorial outposts and political special privileges, the Western Powers will not be deprived of economic opportunity. In the first instance they may lose. China will never again be the happy hunting ground for foreigners that it once was. The Chinese tariff will never again be framed with a view primarily to the interests of foreign traders. Foreign banks established in Chinese ports will no longer exercise a quasi-monopoly of credit. Foreign persons and property will no longer enjoy idyllic immunity from taxation. Nor will they have the most advantageous sites, regulations that work to their interest and to China's detriment, and a multiplicity of priorities as they once did. Nor will they enjoy the monopoly in purveying manufactured goods they once had and counted on having forever.

All that will pass, but it would have passed in any case. It owed its existence to the fact that the countries in the East had not yet industrialized, and it could not survive, once they were effectively industrializing. It was a factitious monopoly at best and in any event destined to be a transient one. Its end could have been discounted in advance. Whatever may be sacrificed in the first instance, however, will be repaid manyfold later by the opportunities opened up by China's industrial development. This development will be accentuated by the withdrawal of Western privileges rather than the reverse and the rewards will be increased in proportion.

The general principle on which any peace settlement must be based is therefore the recognition of a historic shift of power, of a transvaluation in world politics, of a great recession by the states that have been in the ascendant since the Napoleonic wars and the industrial revolution. As between the East and West a new order of relations must be worked out. For one thing, the polar center of world politics will no longer be London, Paris, Berlin, Washington, or any other Occidental capital. Nor will it necessarily be any continent in the Western Hemisphere. This will have repercussions spreading throughout the body of world politics, world trade, and world finance, but they can be beneficent as well as baneful, according to whether the political and economic system set up in the peace settlement is such as to withstand them without shock or dislocation. That brings us to the concrete terms of the Far Eastern peace.

Chapter Five

Verdict on Japan

THE FIRST ORDER OF BUSINESS IN FRAMING THE peace is to deal with Japan. This is not because Japan is the key to international relations in the Far East or because its future position is by itself fundamental to the Far East. Japan's importance is derivative, arising not from its own properties or attributes but from the fact that in recent years it has been situated among weaker peoples and free from check because the more distant states have been immobilized by conflict among themselves. It is the potential possession of China that gives Japan its importance. Japan has been only the last and most dangerous agent in a process that has kept the Far East in turmoil and brought it to catastrophe. If Japan had been destroyed in one of its periodic earthquakes or had remained in medieval seclusion or had never existed at all, there still would have been no equi-

65

librium in that part of the world. There would only have been lacking some of the peculiar and, doubtless, more virulent complications injected by Japan. All this may be true; but it is also true that unless Japan is eliminated as a potent force now, there is no hope of peace in the Far East and therefore in the rest of the world.

It follows as a matter of course that Japan must be frustrated in its grandiose design for a great Asiatic and Pacific empire. For one thing, if it is not frustrated, we shall have no voice in determining the future in that region. More than that, Japan, if victorious, will wield power that by its very existence will call out defensive measures by other countries, measures of the kind that must and will eventually lead to another collision. It will exercise the power in such a way as to necessitate not only such measures but measures in retaliation, thus expediting collision. Japan's intentions in the event of success have been made plain enough by Japan's word and act. The so-called New Order in Greater East Asia which will be instituted will be organized on one clear principle—economic monopoly effected by totalitarian methods. The rest of the world will be excluded, of course, except insofar as Japan chooses to barter for commodities indispensable to itself. Otherwise there will be no Far Eastern trade for the rest of the world. Internally the New Order will operate as an autarchy, with Japan as the dictatorial center. All economic processes and activities will be "rationalized" so as to conduce to Japan's economic monopoly and military power. The outlying areas will not be developed and their people will not be permitted free expression of energy and ambition and hope for betterment. They will be kept as reservoirs of raw materials, their inhabitants living on a peasant-artisan-small shopkeeper subsistence economy, hewers of wood and drawers of water. The Far East will be a closed world, tyrannically ruled by a Japanese dictatorship composed of a military caste and its industrial satellites.

This must be prevented both in the interests of other nations and for the sake of maintaining peace, and it can be prevented only by Japan's defeat. Defeat is not enough, however. Frustration is a negative achievement only. It would serve no purpose just to restore the situation that obtained before Pearl Harbor or even before the

67

invasion of China in 1937. For out of that situation this war has come and so would another. Japan must be reduced to a state in which it cannot quickly resume the role it has played in the last thirty years. All that it has done in those years—and not only in the years since 1937—must be nullified. It must evacuate China completely, of course. It must also evacuate Manchuria and Inner Mongolia; the bogus state of Manchukuo must be abolished and the Manchurian provinces returned to Chinese sovereignty. It must be forced to give up Korea, which should be reconstituted as an independent state with interim international supervision exercised by a commission made up preferably of representatives of minor Powers and a small body of foreign advisers and technical and administrative experts also preferably from the minor Powers; after a stated period, during which Koreans are trained as administrators, the supervisory commission should be withdrawn. Formosa should be returned to China. The former mandated islands and other insular possessions hitherto Japanese should be divided between America and Australia, under mandate if there is a mandate system or outright if there is not. In short, Japan should be shorn of all the gains of its aggrandizement since it started on the road to imperial power. It must withdraw to its own islands, its territorial dimensions reduced to what they were when Commodore Perry's ships ushered it into the modern world. In lieu of punitive indemnity for the spoliation of which it has been guilty, the excesses it has committed—since indemnities commensurate with wrongs done are impracticable in the modern world—all its physical properties and material assets on Chinese soil should be awarded to China as part compensation. All its movable armament must be surrendered, all its merchant marine turned over to China. A generation of aggression must be canceled out, not only as the righting of a wrong and the establishment in the Far East of a relationship of equity but as a deterrent of future aggression.

To the end of laying a deterrent Japan must be not only defeated, but crushed—as has been said, maimed and left helpless, beyond recovery for a long period. This may have the ring of meretricious wartime emotionalism, it may have the ring of the retired colonel and the sedentary editorial writer; but it contains an essential political truth nevertheless. For reasons peculiar to Japan and for the sake of a future without bloodshed Japan must be taught a terrible lesson, a lesson that cannot be conveyed by defeat in itself. To a nation of a martial tradition such as Japan, a nation for which war is in the nature of things and the loftiest activity in nature, defeat signifies only the end of an episode that went wrong. It merely leads to a study of the miscalculations that made the episode go wrong and preparation for another effort with better prospects of success. All that it teaches is the misfortune of losing a war, not the tragedy of war itself or the consequences of aggression. For Japan one round would be over and it would gird itself for the second. All that the other countries would gain by victory is respite while Japan was recovering.

To the Japanese, war has been in the last generation an agreeable diversion. Since 1905 at least it has been a safe and satisfying adventure. They have enjoyed an exceptional degree of impunity, being situated in an area of weaker, almost unarmed peoples. They could invade other countries, wholly immune from any danger of invasion themselves. The fighting has always been on other people's soil. It is other countrysides that are scarred, others' villages that are devastated, with men, women, and children slaughtered alike, others that must live out their lives among ruins and impoverished. For Japan the adventure closes with martial celebrations and emotional satisfaction. It is further corroboration of the superior qualities of the country's military rulers and vindication of their right to have their way. It is further demonstration of the divine attributes of Yamato damashii, the unique and chosen spirit of the Japanese race. There is nothing from which to deduce the horrors of war, nothing to recommend the desirability of peace as such. A few Japanese soldiers are left dead in the invaded territory, but the loss of sons fades out of memory, the more quickly among a people of a warrior tradition. The costs must be defrayed in the form of higher taxes; but among people whose lot has always been meager and must be accepted as apportioned by their masters, this is endured fatalistically. Poverty for the many also is in the nature of things. Otherwise no scar is left on the country, no memory to keep doubt fresh, regrets keen, and resolve firm against repetition. Instead the national egoism is enhanced, the rewards of war are more attractive, rule by a dictatorial and irresponsible military caste is more firmly entrenched.

For pedagogic effect on Japan and for the therapeutic effect in international relations in the Far East the Japanese people must be brought to learn that war exacts a terrible penalty from aggressor and victim alike. They will acquire caution only when they have paid the full price of heedlessness and have always before them reminders of the price. It is not sufficient therefore to break the Japanese armies, drive them out of territory they have invaded, or even force them to surrender. It is necessary to carry the war to Japan and to leave ruins on Japanese soil. It is necessary to destroy the principal Japanese cities and its whole industrial mechanism. This must be done from the air and if we are in a position to win at all it can be done; and it should be done. Much of the country must be devastated, and the Japanese left amid ruins. Thus only can they learn that war is a terrible business. Thus only can the lesson be borne in on memory, and a scarred countryside renew warning that aggression cannot always be undertaken with impunity and that not only others are victims. In any case there will be a long period, certainly ten years, probably twenty years, possibly thirty, before Japan can recuperate sufficiently even to consider revanche or begin to fashion again grandiose dreams of world conquest. It must not be forgotten that even Germany took twenty years after 1918 to recover, with all its industrial plant, its cumulative industrial experience and efficiency, its technological advancement and natural proficiency.

In that interval there may be time for the pedagogic effects of disaster to begin to work. There will be time for disillusion with the omnipotent military caste to gather and for the formation of organized resistance to its traditional dictatorial sway. And out of the wisdom begotten by suffering, disillusion, and remembrance of the cost of military adventurism there may be generated a new temper. And these are the two essentials if Japan is to be lived with at all in the future. The military caste must be shorn of its power within the country and there must be a psychological, even spiritual change in the Japanese people. The two are so interrelated that neither is very likely without the other. But without both all hope or expectation of a revolution in Japan, of a change in the form and spirit of the government and the purpose of its acts, is delusory. It is delusory too, no doubt, to expect that a people can or will change its concepts and its attitudes in a short time, but if there is an interim in which it is helpless anyway and the class that has been the instrument of its impulses is discredited by failure, change may begin to work. But the two preconditions are the wreaking of such terrible destruction in Japan as to give penance some force and the emasculation of Japan beyond hope of striking power for a generation.

Something must be said of the Japanese military caste and the spirit of Japanese civilization, for without taking account of them Japan's national acts cannot be understood or the problem of dealing with Japan grasped. So long as the irresponsible and dictatorial rule of the military caste over Japan is unchallenged and unchallengeable, Japan will terrorize the lands around it whenever it has the physical means to do so and there is no hope of incorporating it into a peaceful international society or of maintaining peace in the Far East. Defeat which leaves that caste supreme is, again, merely a respite. But the reason for its supremacy must be understood. For one thing, it has not usurped rule or held sway by virtue of usurpation. It is supreme by the natural order in Japan. And to describe it as Fascist and attribute its power to the contemporary rise of the spirit of Fascism is to confuse by taking labels out of one institutional setting and pasting them on institutions in a wholly different setting. No Fascism was required to bring about in Japan the kind of internal redistribution of power that has taken place in European Fascist countries. There has been no redistribution of power in Japan. There may have been minor changes in form of expression, but in essentials Japan has been ruled in these recent years as it always has been ruled. This is not variation from normality but normality. The military rule by prescriptive right or rather by right inherent in the Japanese social scheme, the Japanese concepts, and the Japanese scale of values. So far as the political and social objects of Fascism are concerned, Japan had nothing to learn from modern "ideologies."

75

Militarist rule is an authentic expression of the spirit of Japanese institutions and Japanese civilization. And the institution which has given Japanese civilization its form and spirit is feudalism. True, feudalism is not unique to Japan. It obtained over the larger part of Europe too, yet nowhere else with the same results as in Japan. Nowhere else was there so complete a subservience on the part of all except a small caste and nowhere else was the cleft between the classes so wide. Nowhere else was authoritarianism so strongly entrenched.

The emperor worship about which so much is commonly written is exaggerated. It is an effect rather than a cause. For one thing, it is relatively new and was consciously created to a purpose. Throughout the centuries until seventy-five years ago the emperor may have been a sacred symbol but a distant one without much force and, besides, one treated at times with scant respect. The elevation to theocratic significance is a product of the Restoration or the period following the formal abolition of feudalism and the unification of the country under direct imperial rule. It is one of the most successful products of the period. The

76

emperor cult has served its purpose. It has become the magnetic rod which has but to be raised and Japanese of all classes are drawn like so many automatons. And it is used for specific purposes by those groups that have the power and want to wield it without challenge.

The emperor cult is a product of old materials rather than new. Emperor worship is in reality a concentration and transference of old loyalties. The essence of the Samurai code and the basic principle of the feudal system was loyalty to a degree not found in any other feudal system. The Samurai—roughly, knights—were a superior caste, their distinguishing mark a kind of loyalty to their daimyo—the Nobles—which was stylized to an extreme that can be called either fanatic or poetic, according to the point of view. The legends that still stir the nations are woven around the highest exemplifications of this loyalty. Loyalty, however, was the distinguishing mark of the superior caste, the professional warrior. The peasant was equally self-effacing, but the quality of his conduct was submissiveness rather than loyalty. It was negative, as he was negative; it was the obedience of the animal rather than the obedience of a code of human relations.

Toward the end of the Tokugawa Shogunate, in the last few generations before the establishment of the modern regime in the mid-nineteenth century, the traditions of military feudalism had begun to relax. In larger part the reason was the peace imposed by the Tokugawas, internally and externally. But there had also begun to emerge, as in Europe in the Middle Ages, a merchant class. It was acquiring wealth and power but lacked position. It had no place in the social scheme. Then came the overthrow of the Shogunate, following America's forcible intrusion into Japan's seclusion. There followed the restoration of the emperor to substantive power and the formal abolition of feudalism. It was to the credit of the men who guided the country through the difficult transition that they perceived the danger of a vacuum, the danger that lay in the breakdown of one set of traditions and values without the substitution of another. Hence the emperor cult. The old legend of the divine origin of the imperial family was refurbished. A whole body of semimystical legendry was reformulated. And consciously, systematically, the whole was instilled into the Japanese people, the more easily since adoption of universal schooling and recourse to cheap printing made indoctrination relatively easy, especially among a people singularly docile even for feudal peoples. The emperor became the new focal point of the loyalties once devoted only to the Nobles. But loyalty was no longer a privilege restricted to the superior caste. It could be exercised, in fact it had to be exercised, by everybody. Loyalty always had been the highest value in the nation's spiritual scale, but it was now a value set for all classes alike. It is natural, then, that the hold of the emperor cult should be as binding as it is on the whole nation, that the symbol of the emperor should have the force it has. For to most of the Japanese people it represents a step upward in the human scale. Thereby they are taken into the comity of the nation. Thereby also it has been contrived that the mass of the Japanese should be politically neuter, that they should be submissive, supine, accepting what is handed down to them from above without thought, without question, without consciousness that it is possible to question or to think. Certain motions are performed in the so-called Diet, but they are shadow play on a screen. Rather, they are tolerated so long as they do not touch anything vital. The so-called constitutionalism has been taken on as Western clothes have been taken on—to show that Japan can be modern. But both are external only, for show only.

The cult of militarism has much the same origin as the emperor cult. In the days of feudalism the right to bear arms was the exclusive privilege of the Nobles and the Samurai. Transgression of this unwritten law was unthinkable. The sword was the mark of the superior man. His only was the right to die in combat. Then came the Restoration and with the abolition of feudalism and the privileges of the Samurai universal military service was introduced. Everybody was eligible to bear arms and to serve the nation's highest lord, the emperor. Everybody had to do so, but the element of compulsion implied in conscription was subordinate, for universal military service had become a mark of equality and therefore a step upward in the human scale for the whole of the people. It gave the masses greater social dignity and human dignity than they had ever possessed or dared to covet. It is natural, then, that the hold of the army and navy on Japanese life should be as binding as it is, that the martial virtues should be exalted and the practice of the arts of war prized. Militarism arises naturally out of the Japanese scheme of life.

The peculiar evolution of Japan precluded the development of checks against authoritarianism, medievalism, and feudalism such as have begun to operate in other countries which are not culturally primitive. No other country has had so unnatural an evolution as Japan's. Culturally the Japanese were a relatively primitive people when in the seventh century they took over almost by fiat the forms of Chinese civilization, a civilization already fully developed, complex, subtle, and refined. It was a leap from one human stage to another, rather than a graduated, unconscious progression, as with most races. It was perhaps a leap that no race can make, and much that is incomprehensible about Japan, that makes both its attitude and actions seem distorted, may arise from the deep inner discord of a people who are actually in one stage of development but live in

81

another and therefore are always at odds with themselves and their environment.

There is, indeed, something incongruous in the idea of a loose group of independent feudal chieftains taking over the highly organized, complex, thought-out political system of the Chinese and the sophisticated, subtle, mellow philosophy on which it was based. The essence of the philosophy was an intellectualized humanism. The way of life was founded on humanism and an inquiring rationalism. The principle of government was responsibility of ruler for the ruled, and the criterion of his success as ruler was the welfare of the mass of his subjects. The central idea of the Confucian body of political doctrines, in fact, was the inherent right of the subjects to overthrow a ruler who did not rule benevolently, for since the Mandate of Heaven was in the nature of things benevolent he was by definition a usurper and there was a moral right to evict him. And administrators of government were chosen by examinations in history, philosophy, ethics, and the arts, since only the cultivated could understand the precepts of the sages and therefore govern with reason, benevolence, and justice.

What could tribal warriors make of all this?
What they did: incessant clan wars with ap-
palling slaughter, tyranny, and a brutish indif-
ference to the welfare of the people. Few people
have been more callously oppressed than the
Japanese. There was only a Chinese veneer, and
it seems to have remained just a veneer.

On that there was laid still another veneer,
when in the nineteenth century the Japanese took
over the forms of Westernism, including a constitution and a parliament and, more important,
the Western system of production by the machine.
But the old social organization, the old habits of
thought, the old attitudes persisted. So, too, did
the perquisites and powers of the small group
that had ruled Japan always. But there was a
difference now. These perquisites had taken on a
magnitude that gave the ruling group power and
range undreamed of before, power and range as
great as any group had ever had before anywhere. In other words, the Samurai had ex-
changed the sword for the machine gun, tank, and
bomber. A military feudal oligarchy became a
capitalistic feudal oligarchy with all the instruments of the machine age to deploy. The modula-

tions that accompanied the development of industrialism and capitalism in the West, modulations that expressed the egalitarianism of the eighteenth century and the humanitarianism of the nineteenth, were lacking. Instead there was only a concentration of power, exercising unquestioned command of instruments for creating wealth and extending political control but also exercising the prerogatives of an older social order.

The forms of modern constitutional government were a façade; behind them there was a small minority, for practical purposes absolute, a minority which was still warrior in spirit and action—the feudal chieftain of an older age, the militarist of the present age. Behind them, too, was a mass which was inert, voiceless, exploited, and content. The mass was content because it had known nothing else and had gone through no experience from which it might discern that there could be anything else. There had been no slow but sure induction into concepts of human rights such as had preceded the coming of the industrial revolution in the West. There was only a sudden change of name for the old principle on which the

distribution of power was based. The feudal
spirit and not the feudal forms survived, and still
survive. They coexist with rapid transit, mass
production, experimental science, and tanks and
bombers, and are therefore doubly dangerous.
The human relation remained: command and
obedience its first principle. It was not so much
feudalism as feudal tribalism, more primitive
than ever feudalism was in Europe, a dangerous
anachronism in a world in the machine age.
Feudalism in Europe was moderated and soft-
ened by the humanism of the Church, held within
bounds by the precepts of the New Testament.
There was no equivalent in Japan. In Japan
feudalism was—and on the whole still is—simple,
stark, primitive. And though Tokyo may today
have the tempo, rhythm, and external character-
istics of Chicago and Manchester, it is still feudal
in thought and feeling and human reaction. The
stimuli are feudal, the responses are feudal—but
feudal with a peculiar Japanese accent, reinforced
by the power conferred by mastery of the machine and therefore peculiarly dangerous.

It will be observed that most of what has just
been said about Japan could also be said about

Germany. With allowance for certain differences attributable to geography and racial composition there is a parallel. The alliance between the two countries is based on something more than transient political expediency. It is not accidental that Japan consciously chose to model its constitution on the Prussian when after 1868 it sought to modernize the government, at least in externals. German conceptions of authority and the rights of the individual struck a response in the Japanese almost by reflex. Surveying all the systems of government extant in the world in the middle of the nineteenth century, Japan intuitively took the Prussian as most sympathetic to its own spirit and beliefs and desires. And if Japanese militarism has so much in common with the German, that is not because the Japanese sent the officers of their new army to Germany to be trained and brought Germans to Japan as military advisers. They sent their officers to Germany and brought the Germans to Japan because they had so much in common. To both, the military man was at the top of the human scale.

There is a deeper community between the two countries. Each is at odds with its environment for much the same reason. The development of each has been at variance with that of other countries surrounding it. Each has all the ex-ternals of the civilization of which it is nominally a part while out of harmony with the spirit. Civilization may be defined, at least in part, as a body of cumulative restraints, of sanctions, of self-denying ordinances, all aimed at curbing the primitive in man. It is an unwritten compact to waive the use of brute force in human relations even when its use would be advantageous. Japan is part of the Far East and nominally partakes of Chinese civilization, which has set the pattern for all Eastern Asia. But it has never been touched by Chinese humanism and rationalism, by the rule of reason which, if not always and altogether without infraction, has at least set the goal for Chinese. At any rate, the thou-shalt-not's of Chinese civilization are without meaning to Japanese.

Germany is nominally European, partaking of the civilization of Europe. European civilization is a compound of the Hebrew-Christian doctrine, the heritage of Greece and modern science; but that which has given it distinctiveness in the last hundred years or more is the cumulative effect of the English Revolution, the eighteenth-century Enlightenment, the French Revolution, and the American Revolution. And by them Germany has been almost untouched. For that which is common to all of them, that which is their fruit and their effect on the life of Occidental man, is a concept of the rights of the individual as against constituted authority, a common agreement on the limitations to be imposed on authority to the end of greater dignity for men. Whether the result be called democracy or equality or government by consent or liberalism is immaterial; it has operated as a trammel on force exercised by something above and outside the control of the aggregate of individuals. Of all the larger groups of people called European (in which Americans must be included) Germany alone has been unaffected. It has had no English Revolution, no French Revolution, no American Revolution. It has never passed through the process which has been formative for nearly all West Europeans and Americans. The concept of the individual's rights against constituted authority, the concept that there is or can be anything higher than

88

authority, is outside its ken. Of that which Western men call liberty it is unconscious—not so much opposed as unconscious. There is for Germans no such value. There are small groups of which this is not true; the fact that they are so easily singled out by others and so far from the seats of influence in their own land is proof of how exceptional they are. At the same time and for reasons logically and psychologically related Germany is wholly insensitive to and unaffected by a change in the attitude toward war that has come over Western Europe and America. War to Germans is still mankind's normal activity, if not man in his noblest expression. It could not be otherwise, given Germany's development, just as it could not be otherwise with Japan, given Japan's development. Dictatorship, militarism, force without restraint, respect for force as such, submissiveness to authority because it is authority, because command-obedience is in the nature of the human relationship—these are as natural to Germany, as inevitable in the circumstances of its evolution, as military worship is to Japan. This may explain Germany, may extenuate the guilt of Germany, but does not make it less dangerous in the heart of Europe.

Scientists speak of biological sports, meaning variations from type so pronounced as to be outside classification. In the same way Germany and Japan are political sports. Neither is in the comity of the civilization of its part of the world. Both have all the advantages of their civilization without the covenanted inhibitions. Both are, moreover, equipped with all the instruments of power of their time and environment, instruments more deadly because exercised without the inhibitions and restraints their civilization has put on all others in their environment. And since the first criterion of advancement in our time is mastery of those instruments, the result is a dilemma for the rest of the world. On the one hand, the Germans in their sphere and the Japanese in theirs are qualified for ascendancy by the accepted prerequisites; on the other hand they are not in the compact that gives their civilization its unity and protects it from regression to the barbaric.

In point of one essential, immediate, political fact the problem of Germany and the problem of Japan are identical. Neither will forbear aggression, adventures in conquest, war, till the horrors of war are borne on it at home, vividly and ineffaceably. Germany, too, has in the last hundred years made war only on the soil of others. It, too, has been unscathed, save only for the loss of its sons, which can be forgotten. It, too, has not only respect but admiration for the military caste because of its successes and swells with pride in its feats. It, too, will learn disenchantment with war and see the necessity of curbing the military caste when the price of war and the penalty of aggression are brought home to it, when the ruins have to be lived in and the scars are always in the vision.

Germany and Japan alike cannot be expunged from the planet. Both have to be lived with in the future. Both are too tough and too vital by all the standards of modern society to be negligible in the future, no matter what happens. But they cannot be lived with until they are not only defeated but crushed—until they are defeated, acknowledge defeat, and bear the ineffaceable marks of defeat on their own soil. The fatal mistake of the First World War was that Germany, though beaten, was left without scars. In a few years it could convince itself that it had not been beaten but was seduced to lay down arms by the blandishments of Woodrow Wilson. It did not feel the tragedy of war; it felt only the tragedy of not having won. The mistake of the First World War should not be repeated after the Second World War in Europe and still less in the Far East. Japan must be not only defeated but devastated. After that, certain concessions in commutation should be allowed it in the terms of peace, but that subject will be discussed later in a context in which it fits more logically.

Chapter Six

The Future China

JAPAN BEING ELIMINATED, TAUGHT A LESSON, and put out of action, the next order of business is the question of China. The answer follows automatically. It is dictated first by direct logic and, second, by political reality.

The cause of the war in the Pacific, as has been said, was rivalry over China. Enduring peace can come in the Pacific only when the cause is eliminated. A world war had to be fought because it could not be decided by peaceful means whether China should be independent or a colony and, if a colony, belong to what empire. Other world wars will have to be fought until that question is settled once and for all. This war came about because Japan tried to make China a Japanese colony. If Japan is defeated it fails, of course. The solution of equilibrium by the conquest and absorption of China must then be discarded un-

93

less and until some other Power can follow in Japan's path with better success. And this is scarcely practicable in the circumstances that will prevail after the war. In the first place, all the Powers that might aspire to such a role—with the possible exception of Russia, which will be discussed later—will be too exhausted to entertain ideas of colonial conquest requiring a major war. In the second place, China will be strong enough to make that an all but hopeless enterprise. What Japan was not able to do at the top of its form and at China's door no other Power will be able to do after an exhausting war and from a long distance. Solution by conquest of China being out of the question, the alternative is solution by independence.

This is the answer dictated by direct logic. Implicit in it is the answer dictated by political reality. For the reasons already given we shall not have much choice. Possession is nine points of the law in the politics of war and peace, and when the time comes for the peace treaty to be written Chinese troops will be in exclusive possession on Chinese soil. The Japanese armies will have been driven out or forced to surrender. This

94

will have been done by the Chinese themselves,
though with the assistance of planes, pilots, guns,
and perhaps selected military technicians from
the United Nations. Such forces of the United
Nations as are there will be negligible in quantity,
partly because of the difficulty of transport and
partly because they will not be necessary. It is not
man power that has been lacking in China but
the weapons for Chinese man power to use. As
the war ends China will be undisputed master in
its own house. It is not likely, as has already been
said, that the Chinese will then politely defer and
invite foreigners to return and take over their
old possessions on Chinese soil again, though the
foreigners be their allies. It must not be forgotten
that their present allies were those who held
them in subjection before. It must not be forgotten, too, that the foreigners have been driven
out of their possessions by the Japanese. The
possessions were at least temporarily forfeited
to the Japanese. When the Japanese are repelled,
they will fall to those who get there first or, in
other words, the Chinese. The Chinese will have
recovered their own, with intent to keep it. It
will be the part of wisdom to legitimize the de

95

facto situation in the peace treaty, for the only other immediate recourse will be to get the Chinese out by force, which we probably shall not be able to do and which it would be suicidal folly to attempt to do.

In concrete terms, the International Settlement at Shanghai must be restored to Chinese control. The foreign residential concessions at Hankow and Tientsin and the Settlement at Amoy must be returned in the same way. The former Legation Quarter in Peiping, the zone adjoining the old Forbidden City which was administered and policed by the Diplomatic Corps and in which troops of various nations were garrisoned, must be abolished. Extraterritoriality must be given up and foreigners resident in China henceforth submit themselves to the legal jurisdiction of the country as they do elsewhere. Fighting ships must be withdrawn from Chinese waters. Foreign merchant ships must relinquish the right of coastwise traffic except insofar as special agreements are made with the Chinese government on terms acceptable to the government. Hong Kong may fall in a special category. The Chinese might agree to a transitional Anglo-Chinese condo-

minium, with a graduated increase in Chinese
representation on the governing commission until
at the end of a previously stated period the
Chinese take over entirely. Thus by being able
to make the necessary liquidations in stages the
British may feel the inevitable loss less severely.
This is the most the British can expect. If it is
negotiated rather than demanded, the Chinese
may grant it. Or they may grant it if compen-
sated in some other way. But if they insist—and
quite likely their mood will be one of insistence—
Hong Kong will have to be retroceded too. Much
will depend on the spirit in which the settlement
is made. If Western Powers offer to withdraw
voluntarily and declare the principle of permanent
withdrawal inviolate, the Chinese may make concessions as to tempo and method. If not, the
Chinese will demand and then take. But the
principle must be declared at once and set down
in covenants: China is sovereign in every respect.

Its independence restored, China must then
receive help to recover as quickly as possible from
the ravages of war. The margin of superior
strength within its borders that it will have at
the close of the war it must retain. It must not

97

only recover independence but be able to safeguard it. It must become impregnable against encroachment by any Power and from any direction if there should be a renascence of imperialism in any part of the world. This is the only sure condition of peace in the Far East: that China be so strong that no Power will dare indulge in any imperialistic pretensions in the Far East or even contemplate them. Thus international morality in the Far East will be imposed by constraint and breaches of the peace enjoined by fear of the consequences.

Thus there can be avoided a repetition of the sequence of nineteenth-century events that brought on the twentieth-century consequences. The key to peace in the Far East is a strong China, so strong that it will never again tempt as a prize of conquest and invite rival attempts to capture the prize. Under this condition there can and by every reasonable expectation there will be peace in the Far East. Except on this condition there cannot be peace. For otherwise there will be ceaseless friction between China and whatever nation controls any part of Chinese territory; for it is unthinkable that China will remit from its determination to be free of foreign control of any kind. There will be incidents of mounting magnitude until eventually one Power or another will find itself compelled to attempt to do what Japan has attempted to do. Otherwise, too, each great Power will maneuver against every other great Power for priority in China, territorially, economically, and politically until there are incidents of increasing magnitude between them and they come to collision. In short, there can only be a resumption of that which brought on the invasion of China in 1937, Pearl Harbor, and the sequel. For again it must be repeated, since it is the heart of the problem of international relations in the Far East: it was competitive aggression on China that roiled the politics of the Far East, that led to the establishment of rival outposts designed for future advance, that kept armies and navies in a high state of preparation in the Pacific, with all the psychological and political consequences of competitive armament anywhere. But with China united, strong, self-sustaining, and under no obligation to any great Power all this can be prevented—prevented, as it should be, before it starts.

It may seem macabre to discern anything good in what is so horrible as war, but the way in which the Far Eastern war has developed may have conduced to the welfare of all the nations concerned in the long run—if, that is, there had to be a war at all. Seen in perspective and judged by the criterion of the least human suffering, it was better that the major clash was postponed for four years. In other words, it was better that China bore the full brunt of the Japanese onslaught alone from 1937 to 1941. It was better even from the Chinese point of view. In a calculation taken for decades and not just for these few years there was an economy of suffering even for the Chinese, ghastly as their travail has been. For now China may not have to repeat the experience.

That China would have to fight eventually to save itself from national extinction was almost foredoomed. That was China's tragedy and the tragic price of the heedless, fatal folly of nineteenth-century imperialism. For that insensate break from political sanity all alike have had to pay, but the price has fallen most heavily on China, which was not even among the despoilers but a victim of spoliation. This is an obligation that China can with propriety hold against the Western world and that the Western world cannot fully discharge, no matter how much it does for China now, whether negatively by way of renunciation or affirmatively by way of indemnification. Sooner or later, however, China would have had to recover its patrimony by its own efforts. And it might very well have had to repeat the efforts, first against one interloper and then against another. This way it is making the sacrifice once and for all, with Japan as the enemy.

If in 1937, when Japan first invaded North China, some other Power or Powers had come to China's assistance—whether America or Great Britain or Russia or all of them—Japan might have been repelled sooner. But in the first place the credit for repelling Japan would not have been China's; it would have gone to the Power that had intervened. China would thus have been under obligations, which in power politics, as between weak countries and strong ones, can be discharged only in ways detrimental to the interests of the weak. In the second place, the intervening Power or Powers would have been left in exactly the same position in China as before.

China's position, too, would have been the same as before. Relying on its benefactors, it would not have mobilized its full strength in men and resources as it has. When the peace settlement came, it would have been dictated by those who contributed most to winning the war, which would not be China. China would have remained a semicolony, dependent on benefactors, it is true, but dependent. One contender for mastery in its house would have been eliminated; that is all. It would itself not have mastery in its own house.

As it is, however, China bore the brunt alone and in so doing acquired confidence, self-reliance, capacity to fight effectively and a trained army to fight with. If now Great Britain and America come to China's support and help expel Japan, they come as allies and equals, not as benefactors. They are fighting for self-preservation, not for the preservation of special prerogatives in China. They have as much to fear from Japan as China has. China is one of the United Nations. Its leader, Chiang Kai-shek, is one of the allied military commanders, on equal footing with every other commander. China is not a passive agent, something being fought over. It is not only being helped but helping. If there is victory now it shares in the victory, rather than benefit by it at one remove. It is under no obligation and, furthermore, it ends the war with the margin of superior strength in its own borders that will leave the other victors no option as to whether China shall be restored to full integrity. Whereas otherwise China would have advanced only one step on the road to national emancipation and still had far to go, now it has taken the whole course in a single stride. And, from the point of view of the West, whereas there would have been only one step in advance toward the attainment of conditions under which peace can prevail in the Far East, now we arrive in a single stride, fraught with pain and sacrifice as taking that stride may be. There will not have to be wars to determine ownership of the prize of the Far East; there will be no prize in the Far East.

If China is to be made strong enough to forestall rival attempts at intrusion it is not enough that it be freed of all existing alien encumbrances; it must also have positive help. It must be helped to rehabilitate the devastated areas and to re-establish on the soil and in the towns the millions displaced by the Japanese invasion. It must be helped with the means to resume normal economic life and to set up and maintain an administrative organism that will keep the country at peace, free from the internal dissensions that aggravated its weakness and able to relieve the destitution that makes for internal upheavals. This last, of equal importance with China's foreign question, is as much an economic as a political problem. And if immunity to foreign encroachment is a sine qua non of peace in the Far East, so also are the internal unification and reconstruction of China, for without them there must be the kind of weakness that tempts to imperialistic penetration. And insofar as the Western Powers have a vital interest in the maintenance of peace in the Far East, it is an investment in self-protection for them to help expedite China's unification and reconstruction.

For the unification of China there is a better prospect now than there has been for decades— better, indeed, than since the latter part of the nineteenth century, when the fissures began to appear that opened into the disastrous cleavages of the years preceding the Japanese invasion. For this China is, paradoxically, indebted most to Japan. In a sense it is indebted to all the imperialist Powers, even if by undermining its political and social system they contributed to its disintegration. They did so contribute, of course, even in those aspects of China's life which are purely domestic. For any nation that is even partly under foreign domination loses not only initiative but moral health. It becomes dispirited. It has no goal for which to strive, for it is not master of its destiny. It is not a free agent, even in its most purely internal concerns, and all effort seems useless even in those areas of the national life which are technically free from foreign interference. The question of foreign intrusion overrides all other questions; all else is and must be neglected. For one thing, all else must be waived if the nation is to survive at all; self-preservation requires concentration of the nation's whole energy in resistance to complete conquest. For another, the presence of the foreign intruder acts as a divisive force. The foreigner makes it his business to generate and underwrite division. Rival cliques are set against each other, venal individuals are bribed to stir up trouble. It is not an accident that nations under subjection are always more prone to internal schisms and civil war. The reason may be that they have no other outlet for political expression, for the natural urge to be politically effective. At any rate, there is convincing historical evidence that when a nation is laid in subjection to an alien master, poison has been injected into its whole collective life, a poison that has mainly a paralyzing effect.

Thus it was in China. Foreign intrusion made for dissension and accentuated it. But it also provided the elements for an amalgam. What can be called the racial life force of the Chinese is virile and indestructible. It has been tempered and hardened in the fires of some twenty-five or more centuries of a crowded, turbulent, sometimes glorious and sometimes tragic history. It was when the nation's life seemed to be ebbing fastest that the urge to self-preservation began to pull. It was foreign encroachment that generated first nationalism and then the resolve for unification to make nationalism effective. And it was the formal attack by Japan that brought about the relegation of internal differences to the single object of keeping the invader at bay and saving

the nation's life and soul. What the Chinese had
not been able to do for themselves the Japanese
have done for them. The danger of enslavement
showed the need for unification; the war years,
when all else was subordinated to common action,
showed the value of unity. Attempts to destroy
that unity in the future will be undertaken with
greater risk than before, for they will face the
hostility of a compact public opinion. Unity has
become an end in itself. The habit of united national action is being formed. Factionalism, cul-
minating in a military coup, is at least no longer
considered the normal state.

When the country has been unified under a
central government exercising unquestioned authority it can proceed with what is equally
essential—internal reconstruction. By reconstruction is meant modernization of its material way
of life to bring it into harmony with the rest of
the world. In a way this is more essential, for
while unification is prerequisite to reconstruction
it is also dependent upon it. There is something
of a circle here. No country can be politically
stable without the kind of integration that only
modernization can provide, but on the other hand

no nation can achieve such integration until it has political stability. Undoubtedly, however, unification is the easier to achieve, since it is almost wholly within China's own control while reconstruction is not. The way to reconstruction is through industrialization, and industrialization is not just a matter of perception and volition. It requires first and mainly a large surplus capital. Railways, highways, and other means of transportation and communication, a national currency and banking system, a national system of public schools to do away with illiteracy, hospitals and sanitation, harbors, public utilities of all kinds, plant for industries without which raw materials cannot be extracted and natural resources developed, in short the whole complicated and costly apparatus of modern society—this requires an original outlay of capital, of surplus wealth, in dimensions that no country can have that is still in an older stage of economic development. Here, too, there is a circle. No country can industrialize until it has a large fund of surplus capital or credit in equivalent amounts and no country can have a large fund of surplus capital or credit until it has industrialized.

China is no exception. True, it has already made a beginning of industrialization, and for a country to lift itself to industrialization by its own bootstraps is not impossible. By starting on a small scale it can accumulate a surplus which pyramids until there is a sizable reserve as foundation for credit. But this requires time, perhaps decades. And for political reasons, if no other, China has not the time to wait. It must industrialize quickly, if only because only thereby can any country acquire the means of defense indispensable to survival in our time. In this era, man power, strategic situation, qualities of natural character, patriotism, competent leadership—all are subordinate to possession of a factory system, natural resources, a well-planned network of communications, and technical proficiency as determinants of capacity to survive. China lay helpless to Japan because it had neither the equipment nor the ability to manufacture planes, heavy artillery, or high explosives. It will remain helpless before any or all modernized countries until it has such equipment and ability, once the Great Powers have recovered from the war. China therefore cannot wait for the slow natural accumulation of reserves with which to meet the first costs of a national industrial plant. It must acquire capital costs from without. Here its present allies enter.

If a strong China is to the interests of the Western Powers they must help it to industrialize as quickly as possible. Practically this means making huge loans to China. It means giving to China on long-term credit machinery and certain raw materials—the essentials of industrial plant. It means sending technicians to China to assist in installing plants, directing them at the beginning and training men, engineers, foremen, and workmen to take over their operation as soon as possible. But with respect to loans and technicians alike there must be sure safeguards against political accompaniments of the old kind. Loans must be purely financial transactions, being given on the general credit of the country or on ordinary commercial security, as loans used to be made by America to European countries before 1929 and by European countries to America in the nineteenth century. There can be no more foreign supervision and control of Chinese public services, public utilities or administrative organs as a measure of security, or we shall be back where we were, with one country bidding against another for preferred positions, loans being the means of taking positions, and control of governmental organs the means of holding positions taken. Similarly, foreign technicians, whether managing directors of railways or factory superintendents, must be engaged as employees of China, subject to the authority of those who engage them, and not as "advisers" with quasi-independent status and quasi-diplomatic functions, or we shall be back where we were, with advisers as spearheads of advance for each Great Power. The foreign lenders must find their security and their returns as commercial bankers at home do—security in the good faith of the borrower and the worth of the enterprises established by the loan, returns in the form of interest. There will be still more profitable returns, but they will be discussed later. At this point it is desirable to discuss the purely internal problem of China, since the internal problem conditions its political equilibrium and therefore the state of international relations in the Far East.

China, too, has a population problem. It has

been lost sight of in all the polemics over Japanese population pressure, but in actuality China is further from being able to feed its people than Japan. Given the present number of human beings within the territorial bounds of the country, the rate of increase and the country's capacity to produce with existing methods of production, it would be physically impossible for China to carry on except by the operation of the Malthusian law. There must be floods, droughts, famines, plagues, and wars to drain off the excess in order that the rest survive. It is not because of any racial perversity or incapacity that there are periodic outbursts of internal violence. They are the vents for the pressure of unbearable conditions. The Malthusian law operates, but even so a large proportion of the population is barely kept alive; it subsists, but no more. Emigration is no solution; millions of Chinese have already emigrated without any appreciable effect. Relief can come about in two ways only: reduction of population by birth control or by what can be called the reflex action of a rising standard of living, as in all countries which have industrialized, and industrialism itself to increase productivity.

China cannot sustain its population, even when reduced, without the application to production both on the land and in the town of the means put to man's use by the discoveries of science. It must produce by the machine in the town and, on the soil, by what the advance of science has put to the service of the farmer in the form of plant and animal biology, soil chemistry, and machine implements. Only thus can a level of livelihood be provided that will assure contentment for the mass of the Chinese and therefore stability. Only thus can there be found a basis for equilibrium either in China's foreign relations or in its internal affairs. At bottom China's problem is one of social transition, of passage from an older form of society to that which obtains in the rest of the world, passage from the Middle Ages to the present.

Industrialization is prerequisite to reconstruction, but not the whole of it. Genuine reconstruction calls for more than revolution in methods of production and increase in wealth. Indeed, it will contribute to neither internal stability nor peaceful relations with the rest of the world if industrialization is carried out in such a way as to reproduce in China the evils of the earlier stages of industrialism in the West and in Japan. Then indeed there will be only a gigantic sweatshop— worse even than the early nineteenth-century Europe at its worst, for there will not be the restraints that were imposed in Europe by the egalitarianism that preceded industrialism and the humanitarianism that accompanied or closely followed it. The lack of any concept of individualism and individual rights was no serious handicap in China when there was effective clan organization, which provided a measure of social insurance; in an industrial system, when the clan and guild must pass, it would be fatal. The result would be a kind of helotry and eventually revolution.

It solves nothing with respect to internal stability or external peace if there are a few great factory centers in cities such as Hankow, Shanghai, Tientsin, and Canton, superimposed on a substratum of peasants ground by rack-renting, usury, and manipulation of crop prices and urban factory hands working fourteen hours a day at wages which barely keep them alive. Neither the rural nor the urban population will benefit from industrialization. Peasant homes with too many mouths to feed will serve as a reservoir of cheap labor to be drained off into the factories in the towns, as has happened in Japan. Cheap peasant labor will keep urban wages down to subsistence level and the agrarian economy will not be any better off despite increased produce, except that spilling excess children into the cities will keep families from being actually hungry. Peasants will have to pay additional taxes to support the expensive public services of an industrialized society without any appreciable increase in real income. They will be living on a money economy without much cash. The urban population will not have enough income to buy much of the increased produce of the land and the peasant will not have any cash surplus to buy the increased production of the factory. As there will be no outlet at home for the increased production of the cities, Chinese industry will have to resort to dumping abroad, which will provide an added inducement for keeping wages at the lowest possible level on which human beings can live. China will still be on a subsistence economy, even though fewer persons will die of actual undernutrition than now. The

whole economy and social system will be as unworkable as they have been up to the present; in
fact, they will be even more unworkable. Through
the centuries a certain balance has been struck
which keeps China at even keel most of the time
—with periodic seismic upheavals when it fails
to do so, a kind of cycle of internal peace and
civil war. But industrialism with little or no
agrarian reforms, operating on the old principles
of dividing the rewards of labor, will add Western maladjustments to those endemic to the native
system, and the Chinese people will be worse off
than ever.

There must be reconstruction in China, but it
must be social as well as material reconstruction.
It must be reconstruction beginning not at the
point at which Europe began more than a century
ago but at the point at which the West now finds
itself. There must be social reconstruction in-
fused with a new social philosophy, one which
applies the lessons of Western experience in the
last hundred years. If there is complete laissez
faire and favored groups or those which command enough capital to come in on the ground
floor are allowed to proceed with industrialization

without restriction and with unimpeded access to natural resources, the foundations will be laid for an unhealthy, deformed society. It is undeniable that some of the evidence discernible in recent years in China has been disquieting. Much of what could be seen in cities such as Shanghai combined what was worst in the traditional East with what was worst in the West before the demand for reform became effective. The beginnings have been ominous; they portend a profiteer-exploiter paradise. Yet there has also been counterbalancing evidence. There has been an awareness of the mistakes of the West—mistakes perhaps inevitable in the West because the consequences of industrialization without restriction could not have been foreseen—and a conscious desire on the part of influential Chinese groups to guard against the same mistakes. This took concrete form in the philosophy and program expressed most systematically by Sun Yatsen in his book, *San Min Chu I*. In that book there is much that is callow, superficial, and self-contradictory, but it is also a well-reasoned statement for the necessity of preventive control of exploitation. Its essence is social control of economic development, without the rigidity and absolutism common to similar systems proposed in the West: the Chinese are not given to intellectual rigidities.

Both tendencies are running in contemporary China. Which will prevail it is still too early to say. But there is reason for encouragement in the fact that there is already a sturdy protest against uncontrolled exploitation and that the war has both weakened vested interests and awakened a general desire for a better dispensation. In that respect the indications are more favorable than before 1937. The center of protest has not been exclusively the Chinese Communist party; but that party has put most articulately that which is felt even by those who do not share its whole philosophy or accept its whole program. As a matter of fact there have been almost twenty years of social ferment, with the Communist party as the leaven. It is needless to argue and impossible to prove just how Communist the Chinese Communist party is. Is it, or would it be if successful, anything easily recognizable by Marx and Lenin, or would it be Chinese—unique but with Marxist tinctures? This cannot be answered. But certainly the discontent, the articulate discontent, antedated the advent of Communist influence in China and has causes that would have operated had there never been a soviet system in Russia or an international Communist party. And if in some way the Communist party and the Communist idea were now suddenly expunged from the world, there would still be in China social ferment, social protest, and perhaps social upheaval in a kind of elemental reaction from unbearable conditions. But Communism is not likely to be expunged, and unless China takes the course of reconstruction with genuine and fundamental alleviation of life for both peasants and urban dwellers, the Communist party will be the most practical vehicle of opposition to those who hold power and wield it only for the minority. The most serious threat to China's inner unity lies in the economic privation of its people and the defective social organization that produces privation. If there should be cleavage because there is no relief from privation through social reconstruction and reform, the line of cleavage will be between the Communists, with the support of a large proportion of the masses, on the one hand, and an unofficial alliance of industrialists, bankers, large landholders, and their bureaucratic and military supporters on the other. In that case China will in all probability be rent by revolution sooner or later and chaos will supervene again. The waters of the Far East will be muddied again. If there are Great Powers inclined to fish in them, the last few decades in the Far East will be repeated.

Here the question of Russia's future relation to the Far East logically enters. It has been assumed thus far that with Japan eliminated the obstacles to China's independence can be removed by the withdrawal of the Western Powers and thus a basis of stability can be laid. It is self-evident, however, that Russia is in a separate political category, both by reason of its geographical situation and the principles that govern it as state and society. In a word, suppose the United States, Great Britain, France, and the smaller Western Powers do withdraw and Japan is crushed, what assurance is there that that will not just open the way for Russian domination? Will not that just confer on Russia the kind of free hand that Japan has had—perhaps even

120

more surely, since there was always some potential check on Japan, if only by Russia itself? The answer is hard to give, since Russia must remain an unknown quantity until the war is over. Until then it is impossible to say what Russia will be, what it will conceive its role in the world to be, from what political and social philosophy it will derive its mainsprings of action. No calculation of probabilities can therefore be made now for its acts or motives.

Russia may come out of the war revivified for revolutionary dynamism, taking up the role of spearhead of world revolution as conceived by Lenin and Trotsky in 1919. The condition in which Europe and Asia will be left after the war will tempt to the adoption of such a role, and there has not yet been any conclusive evidence that Russia even under Stalin has ever abandoned the aims laid down by the original Bolsheviks. It may only have waived them as a matter of expediency, postponing the attempt to realize them until the circumstances are more propitious. And by the classical theory of Communist revolutionary strategy the end of a disastrous war between the capitalist empires should provide the most

121

favorable circumstances, should be the signal for the overthrow of the vestiges of capitalism and the institution of a world-wide Communist state and society under the dictatorship of the proletariat. This is one course that Russia may take. Or, Russia may come out of the war a tsarist imperialism new-style, resuming the historic, almost geologic push toward warm water—toward the Manchurian and North China coast on the one side. Toward Istanbul and the Straits on the other. Signs have not been lacking of the birth of a Holy Russian nationalism in the last few years, and it will take nourishment from the glory of Russian arms if Russia has succeeded in withstanding the mighty Nazi-Prussian military machine. The third course that Russia can pursue is that of reverting to a kind of socialism-in-one-country isolationism. This at least appeared to be the conception Stalin held of the Soviet Union's place in the present scheme in the years before the outbreak of the war. Which way Russia will go, what it will consider its most promising opportunity, it is impossible to foresee while the war is still in mid-course. But by what it elects the Far East will be affected at least as much as Europe, perhaps more.

There are some grounds, however, for the belief that Russia will not be a complicating factor in the Far East. The principal one is that Russia will not be wholly free to act, even if it should prefer a course of expansion in the Far East, whether for imperialistic reasons or doctrinal reasons. For certain checks will be operative against Russia. The first is that, win or lose in the World War, Russia will come out of the war seriously depleted. It will be near the point of complete exhaustion, if not actually at that point. It will no doubt have a powerful army in being, experienced and hardened by years of campaigning. But the longer the European war lasts, the more Russia will have to depend on supplies from Great Britain and the United States. Its army will be of a high order of military competency but lacking in the means of making war. Furthermore, Germany's defeat and withdrawal will have pulled the bulk of the Russian armies toward Europe, and the disturbed, uncertain conditions in Central Europe and the necessity of restoring some kind of normal order there will absorb all of Russia's vigilance and too much of its resources and energy to leave any surplus for attempted penetration at the eastern extremity of Asia.

Another check that will operate is that at the moment of victory and for some time thereafter America will be at the height of its military power and far from uninterested in what happens in the area of the world in which it will have borne the heaviest burden. America will have a political vested interest in what happens in China, at least a negative vested interest. What it would not yield to Japan before it had really begun to arm it will not be disposed to yield to Russia after it has put together a military machine which at the end of the war will doubtlessly be the most powerful in the world, perhaps the most powerful the world has ever known. And doubtless, too, it will not be in any mood of renunciation, more particularly in the area in which it has suffered most humiliation and perhaps most losses and in which it has the largest direct stake. Also America will have something to bargain with. The industrial structure that Russia built up between 1930 and 1940 with so much sacrifice will

124

have been all but destroyed by the end of the war. Russia will need capital goods, machinery, semi-finished products, and, most of all, credit. The provider will have to be America, and America will be able to stipulate conditions. Words will not be necessary. The Russians will recognize that it will not conduce to greater help from America if they fly in the face of an American prohibition, so consistently and uncompromisingly laid down that the risk of war with Japan was chosen in preference to lifting it. This consideration will emphasize the necessity for caution in the Far East imposed on Russia by its exhaustion, its need to rebuild, and its obligations in Europe. Indeed, if Russia should decide that the time had come to extend its influence, whether in old-fashioned aggrandizement or as the vehicle of social revolution, it is more likely to choose Europe as the scene of action rather than Eastern Asia. For Europe will probably be more open to penetration. It will be exhausted; the masses will be impoverished and embittered; the political slate will have been wiped clean; Russia will at least appear to offer a promise brighter than the reality that has been experienced.

The third and probably most effective check will be that of China itself. It is assumed, for the reasons already given, that China will end the war in possession of considerable strength. Certainly its determination to brook no limitation on its independence and no interference within its borders will be unshakable except by force. China will be no more disposed to waive sovereignty in Russia's favor than it has been disposed to waive sovereignty in Japan's favor. Again it must be said: the Chinese have not fought as they have, sacrificed as they have, just to exchange one master for another. Russia may have the opportunity to take Japan's place and it may desire to do so; but if it tries it will have to expend as much in blood and treasure as Japan has. That it will have any better success than Japan is not likely—except on one condition.

This condition is that it be called into China by one Chinese faction to turn the scale in an internal struggle. This faction could only be the Communists, and then only if they were supported by a large proportion of the Chinese masses, goaded to desperation by poverty and hopelessness in the face of wealth being piled up by a new class of exploiters. This is why the preservation of unity in China is all-important and why genuine social reconstruction is crucial to the maintenance of unity. It is why the question of China's social organization is second in importance, even from the international point of view, only to the question of removing the foreign outposts from its soil. For if in the course of social upheaval Russia is invited in by one party and intervenes not only for its own aggrandizement but in the interests of establishing a new social order, a revolutionary order which by its nature will make China an appendage of Russia, then surely we shall have the renewal of the Far Eastern conflict. In fact, we shall have the conflict with a sharper and more deadly edge, for involved in it and determined by its outcome will be the kind of world there shall be in Asia. By the kind of world there will be in Asia the form and spirit of the world in the Occident will be vitally affected, so much so that the Great Powers in the Occident will seek to eradicate the new world in Asia. On all precedents it is hardly plausible that the Great Powers will stand idly by and watch the formation of a militant, Communist bloc extending from the Polish plains to the Pacific. What is more plausible as outcome is a world-wide civil war on the issue of property versus revolutionary confiscation, the only kind of war that would be more bitter and devastating than the one from which nearly all the world is suffering now. But this whole sequence comes into question only if China be weakened from one cause or another and more particularly if it is weakened by internal schisms arising from economic injustice. The sequence cannot be set in motion if China is restored to independence, strengthened, helped to get the means of keeping strong. Under those circumstances Russia, too, need not be feared—whether Russia be red, white, or neutral gray.

One more question with respect to China remains to be discussed. If China, victorious, possessing a good army and high in spirit, is made strong, what assurance is there that it will not itself resort to aggression and become in turn a menace, first in its own part of the world and then to the rest of the world? China has a population of more than 400,000,000, an enormous expanse of land and a plenitude of resources. What check will there be on it if it becomes modernized? The question has an air of profundity and is no doubt exercising many persons and will no doubt exercise many more; but it can be dismissed. It is not worth serious thought. For purposes of defense China is strong now, as the Japanese have discovered, and will be stronger. For purposes of defense it will presumably be impregnable, which as a matter of fact is highly desirable. But impregnability to attack from without does not constitute a menace to others. In this case it is a form of insurance for others. For purposes of defense China may be strong now and will be stronger later but for purposes of offense it will be negligible for years, probably decades. As a potential threat to Europe and America in particular it can be forgotten in the near future.

Military power in our time, offensive power or power of attack, is in direct ratio to industrial effectiveness and does not even come into question until a high order of effectiveness has been attained. A highly organized factory system capable of producing in quantity and limitless variety; a closely integrated system of communi-

129

cations and transportation; ample resources already in process of development and available in large quantity on demand; a population in which all have had some mechanical experience and some are advanced in technological knowledge and training—these are the attributes of powerful countries and the standards by which military power is measured. Only countries rated high by these standards are even potentially formidable. Success in power politics in our time is above all else mechanistic. The events of the last few years stand in evidence.

When allowance is made for all the impalpable factors that entered into the fall of France—the moral collapse, the palsying of the will to resist, the self-emasculation by internal enmities and class hatreds, the preference of certain influential French groups for German Fascism over French Radicalism—the decisive factor nevertheless was Germany's superior capacity to mobilize the resources of modernity. A large and well-endowed country, superlative in point of industrial effectiveness and organizing ability, met a small country still to a great extent agrarian. The result was almost a matter of physics. Had morale been the same on both sides the final result would not have been much different, although it would have taken longer to determine—unless, of course, German advantage had been neutralized by putting British and Russian might behind France in time, as in 1914. Another example is America. The richest country in the world, the most generously endowed in resources, industrially the most highly organized, and, with the possible exception of Germany, the most advanced technologically, America nevertheless needed two years just to get its stride toward military effectiveness. More than six months after it had been attacked it still could not answer in kind and had to restrict itself to the defensive. And as has already been said, even Germany, with a hundred years of experience in machine production and large-scale organization behind it, needed twenty years to recover from the First World War, although its own territory was unscarred in that war and its productive plant was worn out but intact.

What then need be feared from China, a country which, however numerous in population and vast in expanse, still cannot produce a plane or even minor parts, which has only a few thou-

131

sand miles of railway but cannot manufacture a locomotive, which cannot make heavy artillery or high explosive shells or armored trucks, which has no merchant marine and no navy and no really large factories, certainly none engaged in heavy industry? To talk of China as a menace to distant countries now or in the near future is fantasy or a kind of imitation realism to which many are now prone, mainly in reaction from the wishful thinking especially prevalent in America after 1918. Having grown up politically, many are deriving a kind of voluptuous satisfaction in being more Machiavellian than Machiavelli. The Chinese will no doubt for a time be excessively nationalistic, assertive, even chauvinistic in manner and speech. They will be difficult, perhaps even trying to those who come into contact with them at home. They will give themselves an emotional fling, bent on proving to all others that they have won the right to equality, perhaps bent even more on proving to themselves that they have won it. They will get compensatory satisfaction for years of humiliation, years of having to bend to superior force. This is almost a chemical formula for nations which have newly won free-

132

dom after long oppression. It can be taken as a
fixed rule in international politics and discounted
for in advance.

It has no serious political consequences, however, unless the compensatory satisfaction takes
the form of actual aggression on others. And this
is a matter of physical capacity, not emotional
bent. China will have no such capacity—not for
forty or fifty years, not until it has the industrial
structure of America or Germany or Great
Britain. To plan so far in advance is both needless and impossible. Too much will happen in the
interval that cannot now be calculated for. No
one can make even a hypothesis of what will have
evolved politically by that time. We may have
worked out an international order. New constellations of power may have arisen. In the mean-
time it is wisest to dismiss as Boy Scout stra-
tegics all theories of curbing China lest it become
a Yellow Peril—Chinese hordes overrunning the
planet in rickshas, no doubt. It is wisest to dismiss
as pretentious and trifling the pseudo-Machiavel-
lian conceits of a Far Eastern balance of power,
with China not too strong, Japan not too weak,
so that they can check each other. This could not

be contrived, even if there were any political sense in it. Sufficient unto the immediate future will be the insoluble problems thereof. A Chinese menace is not among them. It is a creation of political novitiates, still thrilled by discovery of old truths, especially the truth that in the relation of large groups power is an entity, a reality, that cannot be negated or wished away by evangelical rhetoric after the manner of the so-called new peace system in the years between 1919 and, say, 1930.

Chapter Seven

Japan's Legitimate Needs

IN THE INTEREST OF LASTING PEACE IT IS NECESsary to put Japan out of action and beyond possibility of early recovery as a military menace; but further than that it is neither necessary nor advisable to go. On the contrary, it will be necessary to take such measures as will enable Japan to live and prosper. In other words, Japan must be left no legitimate reason to cherish dreams of revenge or even in the minds of reasonable Japanese to construe revenge as the only means of self-preservation. Therefore it is useless to consider seriously the various proposals that have been made for keeping Japan permanently disarmed, forcibly overthrowing the monarchy, and instituting a government that will presumably be more law-abiding, and thereafter policing the country to ensure good behavior. These need not be considered because they are not practicable,

and if they were practicable they would work
more harm than good in the long run. They would
require nothing less than the garrisoning of the
country with foreign troops, perhaps the complete military occupation of the country. All the
country's political acts would have to come up
for visa, all its production would have to be in-
spected for approval as designed for civil and not
military use. How it would be determined whether
a steel mill or automobile factory will always be
one or the other is never made clear. It cannot be
determined, of course. Almost any part of the
productive apparatus of an industrialized country
is convertible to military purposes. The only recourse would be to dismantle such of Japan's
industrial structure as remained after the war,
prevent any installation of new plant and keep
the country on a peasant level. This is of course
absurd. The only result even of partial occupation and dictation over Japan's domestic life
would be to solidify the whole Japanese nation
behind the most extreme militarists in a national
plot for rebellion. An incidental result might be
the generation of suspicion of Western motives
in the minds of other Far Eastern peoples. For

136

Japan, too, could serve as an imperialistic spring-board in the Far East. Against this danger the whole Far East will be standing on its guard.

All this need not be considered seriously. It is wartime emotionalism rather than sound political sense. Instead, after Japan has been made militarily impotent political wisdom dictates that certain concessions be made to it to assure conditions of livelihood on a standard it can reasonably expect, so that it will not have to resort to force in order to feed, clothe, and shelter its people. These concessions can be made without jeopardizing Japan's neighbors in the Far East or laying undue penalty on more distant countries. They do, however, entail a certain loss to Western countries. But in the first place this loss can be offset by other gains arising from stability in the Far East and, in the second place, it must be taken if the end desired really is stability and peace.

It is a truism that no nation will remain more passive than its physical weakness dictates unless assured of the means of livelihood. This may have been distorted for purposes of propaganda in recent years by the play on such words as lebensraum, life-lines, population pressure; but in its genuine meaning it is still valid. And it applies to Japan. No nation as large and virile as Japan will long be kept down if its elemental needs are not satisfied. Japan's economic problem must be met, but first it is necessary to understand clearly just what this problem is. There has been —or there was until Japan entered the World War—far too much emphasis on Japan's economic needs as an explanation of its political policies and in extenuation of its attempts to expand by force. Japan's population problem has become a catchword in all discussion on the Far East, so much so as to falsify the issues. Japan's population problem does not differ in kind from that of any other country. It differs only in the degree of its urgency, and this difference is not enough to give any distinctive content to Far Eastern international relations.

The whole overemphasis in recent political polemics on the importance of population is dubious and has had unfortunate effects. Important as considerations arising out of population may be biologically and perhaps sociologically, it may be argued that in international relations they are negligible. It may be argued further that since the passing of the social environment out of which Malthus drew his conclusions population has ceased to be a dynamic of national political movement except in explanations after the fact. What is an overpopulated country in our time? It is one that cannot extract from its own soil the produce with which to feed and clothe its people and also cannot fabricate goods or commodities with which to buy from without the essentials for feeding and clothing its people. This is to say that primitive lands or even technologically backward countries such as China and India may be overpopulated, but not such countries as have entered the system of machine industrialism and are or can be in the world market. Countries in the latter category which lack "living space" are more likely to be suffering from defective social arrangements, not excess of population. In the case of Japan it cannot be denied that the country's economic basis is insecure, but the explanation lies not so much in the ratio of persons to area as in the impediments to the most effective use of those resources. For some of these impedi-

139

ments Japan itself is to blame; for others it is not. But none of them is irremovable.

However, with all the false accentuations and disingenuous apologies stripped off, Japan's economic difficulties must be taken into account. Japan must be allowed and even assisted to find a secure basis for its economy. Just curbing it in aggression is not enough. It will break bounds again and have to be curbed once more unless within the limits to which it is confined its people can find a way of life that satisfies their needs. But in this there is nothing mystical or unique, certainly nothing that justifies or requires the kind of conquest on which Japan has been bent. There is nothing calling for Japan's territorial aggrandizement or political arrangements peculiar to the Far East. All that is demanded and that must be contrived is the removal of any artificial obstacles which curb Japan's legitimate economic activities, which restrict its freedom of purely economic movement. What then is the economic situation in Japan of which cognizance must be taken in arriving at a settlement in the Far East?

There are two fundamental facts that govern the social state of Japan. The first is that it has a population that has more than doubled in sixty years and now exceeds 70,000,000, pent within an area of less than 150,000 square miles of which only one-fifth is arable. The second is that Japan lacks most of the raw materials essential to industrial production. The second is the more important by far. In this respect Japan's state can be described as destitution. For cotton, iron, petroleum products, lead, zinc, tin, rubber, aluminum, nickel, chrome, manganese, and other minerals and metals Japan is dependent in larger part and in some cases almost wholly on outside sources. In silk and copper it is well endowed and of coal it has reserves of some proportions, though good coking coal must be imported. Its situation as an industrial country is therefore almost unique and certainly has peculiar difficulties. In result it can be said that Japan has more people within its borders than can possibly be sustained on the resources of Japan proper. When this is said, however, it must be added that nevertheless there has been since Japan began adapting itself to modernism a distinct rise in standard of living simultaneous with the marked increase in population. There are too many mouths to feed no doubt; but each has more to eat than before there were too many. So far from the increase in population causing a decline in standard of living, it may be said that the rise in standard of living has caused the increase in population. At least there is evidence of profound changes in amelioration at work in Japan, generated from within Japan itself as part of the country's development and wholly unrelated to the country's actions outside itself. For the rise in standard of living, coincident with the increase in population and despite the increase, had set in before Japan had embarked on a career of expansion presumably to find room for its excess population. In other words, industrialization has had the same effect in Japan as everywhere else—increase in productivity and simultaneous increase in population, the curve of the latter first rising steeply and then tending to level off. For reasons growing out of Japan's geographical limitations it has been harder to arrive at a balance there than elsewhere but the movement toward equilibrium is unmistakable. On all precedent Japan's population should be stabilized in size in a few decades.

In any case, however, Japan's difficulties are

142

more complex than is conveyed by demographic explanations, and their solution is not to be found in anything so simple as "outlets" for surplus population. On the other hand, their solution can be worked toward in measures easier to bring about than outlets for surplus population, if by the latter is meant acquisition of more territory. The question whether acquisition of more territory ever works directly to relieve population pressure may be passed over as not relevant at this point. As a matter of fact, it does not. It can yield high material and emotional rewards but relief from overcrowding is not one of them. The main reason is that the surplus population never moves into the newly acquired territory.

Japan's difficulties are not demographic. In the larger part they are of the time, characteristic of all countries that are of the time. In the main they are not peculiarly Japanese. They are unique to Japan and have distinctive aggravations only insofar as the circumstances in which Japan incorporated itself into the time were abnormal and Japan's development as a people has been abnormal. The leitmotiv of nearly all writing on Japan for decades was a note of breathless wonder at the "miracle" of Japan's transformation into a modern state and society in fifty years. Like all miracles, this one could have been subjected to cold internal criticism. In the past it has always been fair to question whether there was a transformation or just a superimposition of a new exterior. Railways, telegraphs, textile mills, a good navy, and bombing planes do not constitute a modern society. Until very recently Japanese institutions had changed but little in reality. They remained the institutions of a peasant-handicraft society with special modifications deriving from Japanese feudalism, and to them were attached the accouterments of the West. These were adjuncts to Japan, however, not an integral part of Japan. Or it might be said that Japan had donned an extra outer garment, but the body and spirit remained the body and spirit of the old Japan. The rest of the world saw only the outer garment, however, and was dazzled.

There are still questions to be put against Japan's transformation but now they are questions not as to fact but as to effect. In recent years the transformation has gone under the surface. Now Japanese institutions really have begun to change. If they are not wholly the institutions of an industrialized society, they are equally far from the institutions of a peasant-handicraft society. Instead of being a peasant-handicraft society with Western adjuncts Japan is now an industrialized society with survivals of peasant-handicraft institutions and feudal forms and a feudal spirit. The problems of Japanese government, business, and finance essentially are the problems of Western government, business, and finance.

Japan has performed its feat, a prodigious one if not miraculous, and now it is beginning to pay the price. The effects of industrialism are cumulative, and in Japan they have begun to tell. Until latterly Japan had had only the advantages of Westernism—wealth, power, extension of range, comfort, and efficiency. Then it began to get the disadvantages—dependence on foreign trade; dependence on external sources of raw materials; burden of armament expenditures to support expansionist policies based on need for foreign trade and foreign raw materials; entanglement in the world economy; submergence of the agrarian population. That Japan has succeeded in adapting

Westernism can no longer be doubted. What can be doubted is that it is any more successful in escaping the penalties of Westernism than the West has been. On the evidence thus far the answer is in the negative. Indeed, to the disabilities inherent in industrialism Japan has added incumbrances of its own making.

The first incumbrance is, paradoxically, that Japan succeeded all too well. Had its progress been more halting, it might have been a healthier country and the Far East healthier too. If it had taken a hundred or even seventy-five years to accomplish what it did in fifty, there would have been time to make an adjustment between the old and the new. The displacement of the old could have proceeded at equal pace with the advent of the new. Instead the new was just overlaid on the old. There was Osaka, with its mills and factories, and just outside Osaka there were peasants cultivating the soil as in the twelfth century, but with one crucial difference—they were also living on a money economy. The old social organization, the old habits of thought, the old attitudes persisted; so did the old feudal oligarchy, but with the difference that has already been pointed out—it had the wealth of a modern plutocracy and the power that comes with modern instruments and weapons. A military feudal oligarchy became a capitalistic feudal oligarchy. The industrialization of the country was parceled out to the great clans after the manner of concessions or franchises. This was not so much deliberate as in the nature of things, which was itself indicative. The decision to make Japan a modern state and society was handed down from above and executed from above, the tasks being delegated to those who always had had power and the rewards being allotted to them. The landed families became the industrial and financial families; it is true that as the nineteenth century wore on and the industrial structure broadened, the base, too, had to be broadened, and new groups attached themselves to the original nucleus, being as it were co-opted. But the principle of an apex of wealth and power remained. There was only a kind of transposition of tokens of wealth and power from land and retainers to bonds and shares in quasi-official monopolies and corporations. And as industrialization proceeded and Japan came nearer to being counted as modern in productive apparatus, the center of gravity rose and the economy of the country became top-heavy.

An economy, like any other body, is unstable when top-heavy. Here lies Japan's weakness, rather than in its surplus population. Nearly half the population is still engaged in agriculture— within the money economy but not yet of it. The rural population must carry the high overhead of an industrial country in the form of its share of taxes for public services, a widely ramifying administration, a military establishment. In many respects, such as the provision of schools, high-ways, electric lights, and other public utilities, it enjoys a standard of living not consonant with subsistence farming but higher. But the proportion of income which goes to sustain these cannot be met out of the rewards of small-scale, hand-labor, subsistence farming. In increasing proportions the small landowners mortgage their farms and become tenants, working mainly to pay mort-gage interest, permanently indebted, forced to tread warily to keep on the line at which life can be sustained. Agrarian Japan is unhealthy, with a malady that spreads through the whole Japanese system. It keeps alive by a kind of cupping—its young being drawn off into reservoirs of cheap labor in factory towns, which in turn keeps factory and other urban wages also at subsistence level or not far above. Thus, half of Japan lives in the social framework of the twentieth century, the other half in the eighteenth century or early nineteenth century at the latest. Except for purposes of production half of the population must be counted out of the economy. For this reason Japan is abnormally dependent on foreign trade. At the best Japan's situation would be difficult because of the necessity of importing raw materials. The difficulty is aggravated because its economic organization does not permit the larger part of the population to absorb the product of industry. In a word, neither the agrarian nor the urban masses have income enough to buy enough of the country's production for the country to be sound. And the correctives found elsewhere in the form of active organization and positive demands by the underprivileged through political parties and labor organizations are lacking, because authority is still strongly entrenched and the habit of obedience or at least passive resignation is still too deeply ingrained. In this way the disabilities inherent in the industrial system press on Japan more than elsewhere. Japan has been compelled to make frantic efforts to capture foreign markets and to throw its system still further out of balance in order to do so.

The second incumbrance of Japan's own making is the insensate chauvinism and militaristic expansionism that have characterized its course since the Russo-Japanese War and that were present in germ almost as soon as the Restoration had consolidated itself in the 1870's. No economic explanation can account for them, and they have contributed most not only to the destruction of much of Eastern Asia but to Japan's own plight, strained as that was even before the resort to war. Indeed, if one knew nothing of the social history of the Western world in the last generation one might conclude that Japan's troubles have been wholly attributable to the fevered attempt to annex the Far East, the megalomaniac frenzy for dominion. As has been said, the larger phenomena evident in Japan are common to the whole industrialized world but in their immediate, most critical aspect they are the difficulties not of an industrial, capitalistic economy but of a war economy. In fact, one might make a strong case in refutation of economic determinism from the evidence of Japan.

Had Japan not surrendered to a reckless career of conquest, it would in all likelihood be sounder today than any other country numbered among the modern and great. It had just come into the stage of industrial effectiveness about 1930. It had for the first time arrived at a position of active competition for world trade, the position from which it made such successful inroads into the markets of almost every other country in every part of the world. Despite the world depression Japan's foreign trade was growing steadily until just before 1937, when it was putting all its resources into preparing for the war with China and the extension of that war which even its most heedless military leaders could foresee as a likely consequence of an attempt to conquer China. Its foreign trade in fact had grown steadily since 1914. Its exports alone, which averaged half a billion yen ($250,000,000) before 1914, had quadrupled ten years later and quintupled by 1936, before the invasion of China. While every other country was seeing its foreign trade dwindle

151

and factories close in consequence, Japan was enjoying an export boom. So far as commercial expansion was concerned, it was going through the most successful period in its history, with the exception of the war years 1914-1918.

Had Japan confined its expansion to commercial advance it might by now have become stable and, compared with the rest of the world, prosperous. Out of the profits of an increasing trade it could have accumulated a surplus with which to finance the extension of productive facilities into heavy industry, thus progressively lessening its dependence on the West. Out of the profits of increasing production it could have paid a progressively larger share in real wages, which would have redounded proportionately to the prosperity of industry through increased domestic demand. As a matter of fact Japan did escape the worst impacts of the depression. It could also have strengthened its foundations so as to meet the present economic crisis solid and secure, perhaps the only one of the great countries to be secure.

These were the years, too, of the inception of nationalism in China and of the beginning of Chinese industrialization. If the relations between the two countries had been amicable, Japan might have profited from both. If Japan had befriended China and, as the stronger of the two, had stood behind it in its efforts for emancipation from Occidental interference and control, leadership in Asia would have gone to Japan without aggression. Japan, the first powerful nonwhite nation, would have been the Asiatic world's shield against the conquering white empires. If then there had had to be war to evict white empires—and probably there would not have been—Japan could have fought on the soil of all Eastern Asia as its defender and not as its conqueror in place of the white empires, a conqueror the Asiatic peoples fear even more than their former white masters. Economically Japan would have profited too. It would have had priority in China's markets, not only because of contiguity but by favor. Where competition was keen and prices were equal or nearly equal, good will would have tipped the scale in favor of Japanese goods. To a certain extent the Chinese have been accustomed to using purchase of foreign goods as a political weapon. Japan would have had good will, and in Eastern commercial relations good will is a prime factor.

Furthermore, if Japan had had China's trust, China would have been willing to contract loans from Japan with which to expedite the building of railways, opening of mines, cultivation of cotton, and similar enterprises. From all of these Japan would have been the beneficiary, directly in getting its raw materials from a closer source, and thereby cheaper, and indirectly in having more of China opened to its exports. Lack of communications has been the greatest obstacle to access to the Chinese market. Instead, however, Japan became the source of the greatest threat to China and China answered with anti-Japanese boycotts. Japanese aggression on China has actually been an economic asset to Japan's Western competitors in China.

Japan chose the course of militant nationalism, aggression, and expansion. Now, nationalism and expansion may be inseparable from industrialism and part of the social setting into which Japan has merged itself. They may even flow from modern industrialism. To a degree Japan's attempts to conquer the Far East followed from its success in reaching the stage of industrial effectiveness. That is to say, it had come to a point where it had to have access to the raw materials to be found on the Asiatic continent and outlet for its products. Even in its more egregious form Japanese lust for conquest has had a certain economic motivation. The fear that other empires would pre-empt the Asiatic mainland and close the door to Japan economically, thus forever stunting Japan's economic growth, had a share in prompting aggression. But it is clear that guarding against this danger and satisfying legitimate economic needs did not require Japan to go to the lengths it did. On the contrary, as has just been shown, both ends could have been attained more effectively by the opposite course—one of friendship and protection for the Asiatic neighbors. Negative measures in restraint of Western empires would have sufficed. Japan was strong enough to proclaim and enforce a genuine Monroe Doctrine, an injunction against further Western penetration in the Far East while renouncing any similar aspiration on its own part. In reward Japan would have had both moral and economic priority. It was uncontrolled militarism, not the economic imperative, that drove Japan on its imperialistic career, militarism uncontrolled be-

cause Japan in spirit still dwells in the feudal age.
In actuality Japanese militarism has been not only
the principal cause for Japanese aggression and
the main disturbing element in the Far East but
the greatest handicap to Japan's own economic
welfare—greater than its excess population and
its poverty in natural resources.

There is a Japanese economic problem, and
Japan has legitimate economic needs. But they
have only an indirect relation to what has been
done politically. They are cited by Japanese apolo-
gists as excuse after the fact of aggression. Solution for both could have been found without doing
what Japan has done and can be provided after
Japan is punished for what it has done and made
impotent to attempt to do the same thing again.
Japan's economic difficulties are not insuperable.
To sustain its people on a standard of livelihood
comparable with that of other modern countries
Japan needs only to go forward with industrialization, free from incumbrances either of its own
making or imposed by others. Without complete
industrialization it cannot feed, shelter, and clothe
a population of more than 70,000,000 on a few
small islands meager in resources; that is clear.

But to industrialize completely only two things are necessary: unimpeded opportunity to buy raw materials essential to machine production and unimpeded opportunity to sell the products manufactured with the raw materials. Both it must have in order to exist; for both it will fight; to ensure both it would be justified in fighting. The peace settlement must be such that there shall be no artificial obstructions to its acquiring both.

Given opportunity to buy raw materials and sell finished products, Japan has such natural advantages that under normal conditions it can not only subsist but prosper. Despite its poverty of natural resources, it has a peculiarly favorable situation. It lies at the door of a continent which has ample raw materials and which constitutes the only undeveloped market of any magnitude left in the world. With respect to both resources and market it enjoys competitive advantages over every other country. It is not only geographically closer but has a racial and cultural affinity with the people of the region; all prospective competitors are distant and culturally and racially different. Japan can buy the raw materials of the Asiatic mainland and sell the finished products to the countries on the Asiatic mainland by normal economic processes. In normal economic competition it can buy the raw materials cheaper than its competitors, since its transportation costs are lower, and sell goods cheaper for the same reason. Nothing except perhaps the hostility its political acts generate can prevent Japan from getting the larger share of the continent's raw materials and the larger share of the market on the continent.

China is Japan's natural economic sphere, and China alone offers Japan enough scope to keep itself not only solvent but moving on a rising scale of wealth for a generation—always on the premise that China is not antagonized by Japanese aggression or threat of aggression. Despite the ill-feeling between the two countries Japan has almost always in recent years had the larger share of the Chinese market for consumers' goods, and the potentialities of the consumers' goods market are by no means exhausted. This trade is almost exclusively Japan's, since it does not pay to transport very cheap commodities from Europe or America. Beyond that lies the real opportunity—that of supplying China's needs for capital and producers' goods over the decades in which China is itself industrializing. While this is not exclusively Japan's market, Japan must get the larger share. In such of these goods as Japan can supply at all it again has the competitive advantage of nearness and therefore lower costs. If China is left at peace, so that it can proceed with reconstruction, and not so embittered that it will operate almost a regime of nonintercourse with Japan, China's market for loans will be open to Japan. Given harmonious relations, China can absorb the whole Japanese surplus capital in loans for its own reconstruction, paying interest and amortization in the form of raw materials. As the purchasing power of China is increased by the reconstruction financed by Japanese loans and more of the country is thus opened to foreign trade, Japan can prosper in proportion, selling first consumers' goods and then producers' goods. The excess mouths of Japan can be fed from China—without sending them to China as an expeditionary force.

While China is Japan's natural economic sphere, the area of its economic activity cannot be demarcated by China's boundaries. There are the neighboring regions in Eastern Asia, most of them until 1941 colonial possessions of Western

159

Powers, with which Japan stands in the same geographical relation as with China. In point of physical fact Japan has natural economic priority, too, in French Indo-China, the Dutch East Indies, British Malaya, the Philippines, Thailand. While in those regions the opportunities as a market are more limited than in China, since their early industrialization is not in prospect they offer impressive possibilities. With a combined population of nearly 150,000,000 they can absorb a formidable quantity of consumers' goods at least. And the tariff barriers and quota limitations that had to be thrown up against Japan after 1930 testify that under free competition they are a market worth preserving, and furthermore are a field in which Japan can be, and perhaps should be, pre-eminent. There, too, Japan has scope for enterprise which can keep its factory wheels turning and its workers employed.

These are natural economic forces in the Far East, and no obstacles can be put in the way of their operation if there is to be peace in that part of the world. This has two concrete applications. First, China must agree to lay no discriminations against Japan, however deeply outraged it may

be by the cruelty of the Japanese invasion; that
is to say, whatever measures China takes to safeguard its economic welfare, whether in the form
of tariffs, import restrictions, limitation of foreign ownership and enterprise, and the like, they
must operate equally against all countries, against
Japan no more than against others. In other
words, China must itself institute and maintain
an Open Door regime—a regime voluntarily decreed and autonomously maintained and not imposed by foreign decision without China's consent,
as heretofore. As a matter of fact this will work
to China's own interest. It is to China's interest
to buy, sell, and borrow in a free market, to be
in a position to "shop around" for what it needs
for its reconstruction. Furthermore, the Chinese
are an old trading people, and while they have in
moments of high tension used economic weapons
for political purposes, incurring losses if necessary, on the whole they are by temperament inclined to look to the main chance. They have had
to do so. Existing on a narrow margin, they cannot long afford the luxury of emotional satisfaction at an economic sacrifice. They would go under
if the luxury were overindulged in, and as they

are a singularly practical people they do not over-indulge—except in times of desperation as after the Japanese invasion. But in any case the provisions of the peace treaties, whether bilaterally between China and Japan or multilaterally contracted with all the United Nations as signatories, should include a stipulation that Japan will not be economically penalized. After it has made partial restitution by the cession to China of all its properties on Chinese soil, as has already been outlined, it will stand toward China on a footing of equality with all other countries.

It goes without saying that no other Power must interpose obstacles. With respect to China the question does not arise. With China independent the other Powers will have no opportunity to determine its economic relations with any other country. If there are any inequities in China's international economic relations they will be of China's own making. Open Door in China, partially Open Door, Closed Door—China will decide; actually, however, there is little or no prospect that China will seek to close its door, since it needs too much from outside. The Western Powers will have voice only toward persuasion of

China that exclusion of Japan will not conduce to peace in the Far East and China's own interests —if the Chinese need persuasion. The question does arise, however, with respect to the rest of Eastern Asia or the regions over which the Western Powers have had political control and presumably will continue to have political control at least for a period. The political readjustments called for in those regions will be discussed in the next chapter. But economic readjustments will be called for, too, and they will have to be such as to operate to Japan's benefit and entail proportionate sacrifices by the Western Powers. In a word, the Western Powers will have to stand by while the bulk of the trade of those regions goes to Japan and take no steps to interfere in their own behalf.

Insofar as Japan had even the color of a legitimate grievance before it set out on the last phase of its career of conquest, the grievance turned on the barriers that were thrown up against it in the Western colonies in Eastern Asia. By tariffs, quota agreements, and other devices Japan was prevented from getting as much trade as it would have got in normal competition. While it is true that despite these barriers Japan was getting an increasing share of the market and gradually displacing even the sovereign countries, so great are its geographical advantages, nevertheless arbitrary limits were imposed against it by virtue of the fact that distant empires exercised sovereignty. And as a matter of fact the barriers worked to the detriment of the native populations, too. The level on which these populations live is such that they must buy either cheaply or not at all, and only Japan can lay down goods cheaply enough. It must be repeated, it does not pay a distant country to transport cheap commodities halfway across the world, or, if such goods are shipped, transportation costs bring their prices above the purchasing power of most of the natives. Therefore, the natives must be able to buy Japanese shirts or shoes or bicycles or dishes or farm implements or they cannot buy them at all. If Japanese shirts and shoes are kept out by tariff barriers, they must go without shoes and shirts or have fewer; certainly they must go without things of a higher price level, such as bicycles, tinned foods, implements. Essentially what is in operation is a dog-in-the-manger regime.

The Powers now sovereign in the colonies of Eastern Asia must abandon that policy. It is necessary to extend most-favored-nation treatment to Japan in each colony or at least in stages to dismantle the tariff barriers raised against Japan. And the quota agreements must be dropped or modified in the direction of greater liberality to Japan. The effect will be, of course, the eventual economic displacement of the empires by Japan in their own colonies; in consumers' goods displacement will come at once. This may be regrettable and costly, but it is inevitable in the natural course. It is ordained by geography and in the movement of history. It is an accident of the disparity of military power and social effectiveness in the nineteenth century that Western Powers were able to acquire sovereignty on the other side of the globe in the first place. The disparity is now being redressed and continuation of sovereignty is both a political and economic anomaly. Only superior military force or the threat thereof can keep Eastern lands in the Western orbit politically and economically, once there is a single Eastern people that is physically strong and economically efficient. Only superior military power, in other words, can withstand the natural force of time and place. No Western country will be able to exercise such overwhelming military power for very long in the East. The economic rewards of Eastern Asia must go to Japan, since Japan is of Eastern Asia and is economically advanced. They will continue to go to Japan as long as Japan is the only land in Eastern Asia to be industrialized—unless arbitrarily estopped by Western empires, in which case Japan will break bounds again sooner or later. This means in effect that Japan will get first access to the raw materials of Eastern Asia and the first cut in its market. It will and can get them, incidentally, without "manifest destinies" brewed in the minds of army philosophers and "southward drives" in the minds of navy philosophers. It will and can get them without imperialistic conquest on the pattern of the last thirty years, and in so doing will be secure in its economic system, secure in the world.

By any normal calculation Japan should have enough scope in Eastern Asia to occupy its population in gainful employment and thus solve what is called the Japanese population problem. This does not mean that it can and should be excluded from other continents. It should have the same opportunity elsewhere in the world to buy and sell that any other country has; what this opportunity is will depend, of course, on whether the channels of international commerce are reopened and trade flows with relative freedom as before 1914 or postwar conditions constrain the nations to resort to official and unofficial controls as in the years before 1939. In either case the principle that must obtain is equality for Japan. Under a regime of equality Japan may have unnatural advantages for a time on account of its low labor costs. In the first place, however, it is doubtful whether this is enough of a differential in itself to counterbalance the higher transportation costs required to lay down goods in Europe and America. In the second place, the differential is a transient one if, as must be assumed, there will be change within Japan. There is ground at least for such an assumption if Japan loses the war. If there is no dictatorial regime in Japan after the war—and if there is, measures in penalization can be taken by other countries—Japan should follow the course of evolution which has been followed by every other industrializing nation. Labor will organize and

167

demand a more liberal share of the yield from the nation's production. As Japan comes into closer competition with other producing countries it will be found there as elsewhere that in the long run sweated labor is not efficient labor, that shorter hours and higher pay make for larger output. In the normal course Japan's trade advantage based on cheap labor should pass, and in the period of transition only such tariff provisions should be made as are necessary to equalize the difference in labor costs.

These are not movements in a social vacuum, however. They entail sacrifices on the part of Western Powers, sacrifices of trade they now have in Eastern Asia and, still more, of potential trade they had counted on in that part of the world, trade in continuously increasing quantity and value as throughout the nineteenth century. These are sacrifices not willingly borne at any time and still less easily borne when the economic plight of Western countries will be as it can be expected to be after the war. But they must be made; they would have had to be made sooner or later in any case. This, too, is decreed by the movement of history. As it would be the part of Canute to try to keep a monopoly of the East politically once the seeds of nationalism had been sown world-wide, so it would be the part of Canute to try to keep a monopoly of the East economically once Eastern countries had started themselves to industrialize. The expectation of permanent monopoly, with perpetually increasing gains, was a delusive one at best, as we now perceive. It may as well be abandoned once and for all, especially now when there is the added inducement that thereby we lessen the danger of war—or, rather, because unless we do we are certain to be plunged into war again.

There is less of a dilemma than appears. Renunciation of economic monopoly, even economic priority, in Eastern Asia need not necessarily mean an absolute reduction in returns from the East for Western countries. The losses from surrender of priority may be offset by returns from the economic development of Eastern Asia; that subject will be discussed later. But even if they are not, the choice is still between accepting the loss and perpetuating the war system. The loss may, indeed, be one that we cannot bear. Whether the proper functioning of the existing economic system requires continuous expansion of opportunity and extension of market cannot be established beyond dispute. If it does, the choice lies among chronic war, economic decline for the West, or a recasting of economic institutions in the West. That the latter can be escaped entirely can still be believed by few thinking persons. But if it is escaped it will be despite the fact that the expectation of a perpetual monopoly in the East, the expectation, further, of a monopoly of ever-rising profits, must be written off in time; not at once, as it happens, perhaps fortuitously, but in time. That is nature's decree.

Thus far only the incumbrances imposed from without have been discussed. Those of Japan's own making must be removed, too; they have been of greater weight. That which has been represented by Japanese militarism and the squandering of the nation's substance in military adventures and preparation for adventures will be lifted in the natural course if Japan is defeated. It has been stated as a condition of the peace settlement that Japan must be left without power to renew aggression for a long time. There is also the handicap of Japan's internal organization—a nation half-mechanized, half-feudal. As in China, industrialization is not enough. There must be social reform too. Japan cannot on its upper levels function as the Ruhr, Detroit, and Lancashire and at its base as a system of contiguous medieval villages. Nor can it keep a highly productive apparatus occupied in exports alone. Japan's weakness now lies in its abnormal dependence on foreign trade. This is a consequence not so much of its geographical deprivations as of the disinheriting of the mass of its people, rather of their exclusion from economic life. In other words, there is necessary, too, a redistribution of income within Japan. The peasant cannot be kept on a subsistence level and the urban factory worker on the wage level of the handicraft artisan. Economically the depressed classes must be permitted to rise in the social scale.

There must, then, be reorganization within Japan as well as opportunity outside Japan, if Japan is to rest on a solid foundation and free of the temptation to conquest as a short cut. For Japan's population problem, that which at least in profession motivates its political conduct, is social as much as biological, internal as much as

external. But if the rigid scheme that has pre-
vailed until now is broken through by defeat, if
the fixed hierarchy with the militarist and the
feudal, capitalistic oligarchy at the top is shaken,
there is a fair prospect for enforced reorganization. The morrow of a defeat is propitious for
upheavals everywhere and the ruling classes will
come up for accounting. There may still be too
little substance in Japanese discontent to bring
about results; but it is doubtful, too, that the
ruling classes, tumbled from their pedestal by a
humiliating defeat that also carries ruin for the
whole nation, will return to it easily or soon. A
new force will have been set in motion in any
case, and Japan may at least try to fall in step
with the modern world.

Beyond that Japan's future is as the future of
the West, insofar as its economic environment
is already of the same conformations as that of
the West. Production and distribution of goods
by machinery will not exempt Japan from internal
difficulties, as it has not exempted the West. It
will allay some difficulties and raise others equally
serious. But these are not distinctively Japanese
difficulties; they are common to all of the world

embraced in the industrial revolution. Whatever the evolution of industrial, nationalistic, capitalistic society holds for the West it holds for Japan, too. What that is can hardly even be conjectured in the middle of a world war. Having thrown itself into the stream of Western material civilization, however, Japan must be carried along with it. But purged of its anachronistic survivals within and given assurance of conditions of livelihood by economic scope without, Japan can at least be liberated from the demoniac drive that has carried it and the world along with it to catastrophe.

Two questions remain to be cleared up. If Japan is devastated, as has been proposed, how then will it be able to resume manufacturing for export, even to the extent of displacing Western industrial countries, as also is envisaged? For one thing, it will not be able to do so at once, and it is not desirable that it should do so at once. Too quick a recovery would negate the pedagogic effects of the crushing defeat. But it can return to normal economic life at a steady, if not fast, pace out of its own inner vitality. No nation can be ruined entirely, no people completely paralyzed.

Its engineers will not have forgotten how to organize a factory, its workers how to operate a machine. Not every building, not every depository of raw materials will have been destroyed. The urge to live asserts itself in people less determined and vital than the Japanese. Furthermore, Japan will need foreign help to get its industrial plant started again and should receive help on evidence of good behavior. Much will depend on the political cast of those who take leadership in the post-war government and on the indication they give of their purposes. Enough is known about Japan so that judgments can be made about certain groups and individuals. If they are such as to inspire confidence in Japan's desire to become a member of good society, help should be forthcoming freely and soon—but so paced that it can be suspended at once on evidence of regression, without enough harm having already been done.

The other question follows logically: will Japan thereby recover and go on the rampage again? This has been dealt with in another connection. Nations do not recover so quickly from a really disastrous war. They may recover for purposes of keeping their people alive but not for purposes of resuming a military offensive. Besides, there will be China as check, not to mention Russia. Japan will recover fully in time; but as was said of China, by then there may be a new international order, with effective devices for dealing with one nation's aggressions, and in all likelihood there will be new constellations of power, a new center of gravity. In any case there will be pause for a generation.

Chapter Eight

Settlement in Southeastern Asia *

CHINA HAS BEEN THE FOCAL POINT OF THE FAR East and will remain so. It has long been a truism that as China goes, so will the rest of the Far East go. If China is secure and stable and if at the same time Japan is subdued but economically sound, there is a solid basis for stability and peace throughout the Far East. No settlement will be complete, however, that does not take account of the colonial areas in Southeastern Asia to which reference has already been made. The whole region from Hong Kong to British India has been torn from the political fixities of at least fifty years by the spread of the European war to Asia. Hong Kong, French Indo-China, Thailand, Burma, the Philippines, the Netherlands East Indies, British Malaya, and British and Dutch

* Parts of this chapter have appeared in an article by the author in *Foreign Affairs* and are reproduced with the consent of that periodical.

176

Borneo are now held, as it were, in escrow, to be distributed according as the war goes. The process of distribution will be but one of the less vital but more difficult tasks in the making of the peace.

Simple restoration of the status quo before 1939 will not be enough. Too much has already happened. On the contrary, it can be held as certain already that, however decisive the victory of the United Nations, Southeastern Asia will never again be politically what it was before 1939. What is involved is not just a matter of driving out the Japanese and reinstating each of the empires in the colony from which it was dispossessed by Japan. Japan and the United Nations are no longer the only parties to the struggle for possession. In each of the territories in question there is a third party to the struggle—the native population. It can be taken for granted that the third party will not remain passive. In the general peace settlement there will have to be undertaken a thorough readjustment in Southeastern Asia no less than in the Far East proper and in Europe.

The change in the relationship between great empires and their colonial dependencies which began after the First World War will be carried a step further after the Second. In 1918 it could not be foreseen that colonies which were inhabited by people of a relatively high order of national consciousness and cultural development were never again to resume the status they had formerly occupied. But by analogy we can now foresee that the same pressure for change will again be at work, though one stage further down in the scale of national consciousness and cultural development. The colonies on that level, formerly passive, will refuse to accept their former status. Among them are nearly all of the colonies in Southeastern Asia.

In discussing nationalism in China it was pointed out that the First World War had brought to a head certain ideas that acted as political solvents. Perhaps all great wars do, and in that sense all great wars are subversive. In any case the First World War was irreparably disruptive of imperial relations. Nationalism, self-determination, democracy, and other concepts inherently incompatible with imperial rule received marked impetus and in result, as has been said, the war was followed by colonial revolts in every part of the world. On the whole, however, only the

178

colonies inhabited by more advanced peoples were able to assimilate and act on the doctrines first expounded by Wilson and then given a peculiar edge by Lenin. In Southeastern Asia, however, there was little change. For one thing, the colonies there were possessions of Powers which had never been seriously shaken and which emerged victorious in the end. The Netherlands remained neutral. The United States was never in difficulties. Great Britain and France fought on the defensive for three years but their defeat never seemed really imminent; moreover, since Japan was their ally, they were never under attack in the East. On the contrary, even in the worst years Great Britain and France had added to their colonial holdings.

Southeastern Asia itself was little touched by the war. There was no destruction there. There was some economic dislocation but no deprivation. Some areas which exported primary products actually prospered. On the whole, then, the colonies of Britain, France, Holland, and the United States in that part of the world felt the war at one remove only. Perhaps most of all, those Powers never appeared to be in such des-

perate straits, never were so near defeat and
humiliation, that the legend of their invincibility
could be seriously questioned by the native peoples. Again, it is by this legend of white invincibility that the empires have ruled. The legend has
been more effective in keeping native discontent
quiescent and warding off challenge than the
actual physical force maintained in the colonies.
While there did develop in certain parts of Southeastern Asia after the war a nucleus of nationalistic disaffection in reflection of what was taking
place in China and India and in response to stimu-
lus from the Communist International, it remained only a nucleus in contrast to what was
happening in more highly developed regions and
as such it was suppressed relatively easily.

It is far otherwise now. There is war in Southeastern Asia and its impact has been felt directly
by all the native inhabitants, colonial or independent. Many of them have been killed or driven
from their homes impoverished. Possession and
rule have changed hands. Traditional ties have
been severed. The first requisite of an empire—
the ability to protect the subject peoples—has not
been met. On the contrary, each of the empires

has been evicted, at least temporarily, and its native subjects have been left to the mercy of the invader. The prestige of the sovereign is gone. It is not gone irretrievably and in a measure it may be regained by final victory; but it will never again signify just what it did before. The memory of the surrender of Singapore to Asiatic troops and the humiliations publicly put upon white residents by the Japanese everywhere will not easily be effaced from the consciousness of Asiatic peoples.

The Japanese will make little headway with their propaganda of "Asia for the Asiatics," because from Bombay to Vladivostok it has long been recognized that in the vocabulary of Japan the phrase means Asia in subjection to Japan. But in its inverse interpretation, as signifying Asia *not for Occidentals,* the propaganda will be devastatingly effective. The right of the Western empires to rule has been impaired by the demonstration of their inability to rule or at least effectively to repel a challenge to their rule. Even in victory they will return with their glory tarnished. It will have been shown that they *can* be defeated and, moreover, that they can be defeated by nonwhites. What the Japanese have been able to do others will feel that they, too, may be able to do. White empires will not again be able to rule by symbol only. Their power to command will be in proportion to the force they display. The sanction of moral authority has been lost. At the best there will be disaffection and a demand for more rights of self-government; at the worst there may be revolts.

Some distinctions must be made at this point. Southeastern Asia cannot be discussed as a single entity. It is not a unit at all. It is composed of a number of parts with as many variations as there are parts. What is common to all its parts, beside their geographical situation, is that all of them except Thailand have been under alien control. In different degrees all feel an aspiration for emancipation and independence. This has created only a sort of negative unity, however, although someday it may be enough to serve as a basis for joint action against the common enemy—the Western empires. In almost all other respects the peoples of the region differ from each other. Indeed, the differences are on the whole greater than the similarities. The component parts must therefore be discussed singly.

Hong Kong has been taken up already in connection with the settlement in China. It may be possible to set up a transitional joint Anglo-Chinese administration on a basis of recognition of Chinese sovereignty and formal agreement on the date of complete retrocession to China. If this raises too many difficulties with China it will be necessary to return the island to China at once. If provisions can be made to cover the liquidation of British interests there without undue loss immediate rendition would be better. Burma also is in a separate category, since it is part of the larger problem of British relations with India, and whatever comes in India will be reflected in Burma, whether the eventual settlement comes by compromise or after an open struggle. The elements of the problem are the same in both countries, although they have different pitches of intensity. The extent of disaffection in Burma was mordantly revealed in the fact that when the Japanese attacked, the Burmese were at the best coolly detached, and at the worst benevolently neutral—benevolent to the Japanese—or even overtly acting in support of the Japanese. Furthermore, the moral effect of the entrance of Chinese troops in an attempt, abortive as it proved, to stiffen up the slender British forces will be an abiding one. For Oriental troops to be called on to bolster up the Raj in the part of the world where the Raj has been symbol and embodiment of omnipotence will have not only a psychological but a political effect. And the contrast between the Chinese, who held out against the Japanese for more than four years, and the British, who held out for less than three months, also will not be lost on the people of the East. The analogy is not really sound, of course, since Great Britain was already fully engaged in Europe and Africa when attacked by Japan, but emotions, not logic, will determine reactions in the East, and the political consequences will be unaffected by whether the analogy is sound or unsound. It must be recognized now that the repercussions of China's role in the war in Asia will be felt throughout the East for a long time, and they will not be such as to make the position of white empires easier. However, the solution for Burma will be corollary to the solution for India, and the

184

problem of India is outside the scope of this book. But it is not beside the point or reckless as prophecy to say that any expectation that the relations between India and Great Britain can ever again be as they were before 1941 is delusory. There can be compromise or there can be formal warfare, but in either event India and Great Britain will stand to each other in different case from what has ever been before. And Burma will be decisively affected by whatever that happens to be.

The Philippines fall in a special classification and with respect to them there is little new to be said now. In the normal course of events, as envisaged before 1941, the Philippines were to have become an independent nation in 1946. On all the evidence discernible in this country in recent years that was a matter of settled American policy. What still remained in question was the precise nature of the transitional measures to be devised to ease the shock of economic separation for both parties. The Philippine economy had become so closely articulated with the American, the dependence of Philippine products on the American outlet was so great, that to put the Philippines at once on the same basis as all other countries with reference to American tariffs would have undermined the whole economic structure of the islands and with it the position of the government. This had already been recognized and the principle of extending the period for adjustment had been accepted. What still was to be settled was how long the period should be and how the graduated rise of American tariff rates on Philippine products should be paced. But this was a matter of detail and was to have been decided in joint conference after 1946.

If it was settled policy before the war to give the Philippines their independence, it is hardly conceivable that we should reverse ourselves now. Without any wartime rhetoric, it can be said that the Filipinos have earned their independence. They joined in the defense of their homeland without hesitation or equivocation and played their part more than creditably. Even if it were not simple justice to redeem our pledge, it would be reckless for us not to do so, for if the Filipinos were insistent on the right of sovereignty before the war they will be intransigent after it. They have fought for it, and if we were to deny it to them we should be faced with the necessity of suppressing them by force. It is hard to believe that the American people would be willing to undertake that task, especially in light of their previous attitude.

Furthermore, with Japan defeated and reduced to impotence for some years, many of the grounds for such mental reservations as existed before about independence, both among Filipinos and Americans, will have disappeared. Both had been fearful about what Japan might do when the Philippines could no longer call on American support. At least for a period after the war there will be nothing to fear on this score, and in that period the Filipinos can train their citizens for defense and lay a solid foundation for the country politically and economically. And while the United States might have been justified before in taking the position that if the Filipinos want to sever the tie to the United States they must take the responsibility of defending themselves by their own efforts alone, in the light of the war it would be no more than just for the United States to give the Philippines a guaranty, to proclaim publicly that an attack on them by any Power will be

187

construed as an attack on the United States. If the Filipinos offer in return to allow the United States to maintain a naval base in their waters, as quite likely they may, so much the better. But it is a question whether even that need be insisted on as a condition to Filipino independence. It might even be given more readily if we did not demand it. With the lessons of the first year of the war in mind, the Filipinos are more likely to subordinate *amour propre* to considerations of safety. In any case, it seems safe at this stage to say that the future of the Philippines has already been determined by the course of events.

The Thailand problem is also relatively simple. There really has been no problem of Thailand for a generation, or since France and Great Britain came to a tacit understanding on the delimitation of their respective territorial ambitions in Southeastern Asia. That understanding poised Thailand between the two empires, not quite as a buffer state but as an area "out of bounds" for penetration by either. In that period it has done much to make itself secure in its own right. A sense of national identity took form. Modern ideas flowed in. No question of Thailand would have arisen,

188

then, if the whole area of Southeastern Asia had not been unhinged from its traditional structure by the collapse of France and the irruption of Japanese troops. And it will settle itself automatically once these troops have been driven back to their islands. Thailand can be reconstituted again as a sovereign and independent state, more or less as it was before. If stability is to be achieved in that crucial part of Asia there should be no talk of penalizing Thailand for having apparently allied itself with Japan, at least to the extent of granting Japanese troops free passage into Malaya. It could not help itself. The alternative would have been destruction of the Thai cities, and then the Japanese would have forced their way through in any case. True, Thailand took advantage of France's helplessness and vacillation, and with or without Japanese instigation wrested certain border areas from French Indo-China. But it is also true that these areas had once been a part of Siam and had been seized by France in the days of Occidental imperialistic aggression early in the century. They have constituted a kind of Siamese irredenta ever since. If there is to be a general settlement in Southeastern Asia there must be a rectification of frontiers between Indo-China and Thailand, and an equitable rectification would be to Thailand's advantage. On any impartial adjudication it would be awarded all or most of the areas in question. Apart from this adjustment Thailand can and should be restored to the status quo ante.

There is no satisfactory solution for Indo-China. The population of Indo-China, numbering more than 23,000,000, does not consider itself Chinese and never was an integral part of China. Although its numerous rulers had paid tribute to the court in Peking and the cultural influences have been Chinese, the relations between the component parts of what is called Indo-China and China proper never had been close. The rendition of Indo-China to China would not be an ideal solution either ethnically or politically if it were made by outside fiat rather than voluntarily by plebiscite. Whether on open plebiscite the inhabitants would choose to be returned to China is doubtful, and it is possible that if they were the result would be to exchange one kind of friction for another. There is also France to be considered, and presumably we shall not want to deal

190

with France as a conquered province. The least objectionable way out of a situation that offers no way out for which a wholly sound argument can be made is restitution to France but on explicit conditions.

The population of Indo-China has never been reconciled to French rule, which as a matter of fact has been unenlightened except insofar as it has lacked the social arrogance that has characterized British rule and that has done more than anything else to embitter the people over whom Great Britain rules. This has been far more important than any of Great Britain's political or economic colonial policies. Indo-China was not immune from the nationalistic sentiments which penetrated the East after 1918 or from the influences of Chinese nationalism in the period between 1923 and 1928. Communist propaganda crept in also when the Third International was trying to strike at the capitalist empires through their colonial possessions. Serious uprisings occurred, especially after the Chinese nationalists had won a measure of success with the help of Soviet Russia. As a result, in the period before and after 1930 the French had to resort to drastic punitive measures to suppress disaffection. Indo-Chinese nationalists were hunted down and killed or driven to cover. The measures taken were so drastic as to leave considerable rancor.

The contemptuous treatment accorded the French by the Japanese and the submissiveness of the Vichy proconsuls to brusque commands of Japanese generals have not enhanced the esteem in which the French are held by the native population or their moral authority. It is true that France had already made some concessions to native sentiment before 1939, and made even more thereafter; but still more will be required. Even though its rule is reinstated, France can maintain its rule only if it makes a definite effort to conciliate native sentiment. There must be a sharp increase in native representation in government at all levels in the administration. Natives must have a voice in the making of policy. Those with educational qualifications must have opportunity for minor professional and white-collar posts in the civil service and opportunity to win promotion. No one thing has done more to stimulate native disaffection in colonies everywhere than what can be called the occupational pale—the rule, written or unwritten, whereby natives are restricted to the lower ranks in the public service. They can be clerks, overseers, supervisors, the civilian equivalents of noncommissioned officers—but seldom officers. Thus the first nucleus of discontent has been formed almost everywhere. It is not accidental that the first recruits to native nationalist movements are from the young men of the educated middle classes. Indo-China, moreover, must have more local autonomy. More educational facilities must be provided. Economic and tariff policies must be devised with more regard for native welfare. In short, there must be consistent, perceptible devolution of power from the top and a broadening base of power at least in the middle ranges of the population. Since this would represent a reversal of French colonial policy as a whole, it will not be easy to bring about. But unless brought about, Indo-China, even though restored to France, will not long remain French. The nationalists of the region will rise again and they will have moral encouragement from China, if not material assistance.

With regard to the Netherlands East Indies restitution to the Netherlands is the only practical

193

course to follow after the war. There is not yet in the islands which constitute the colony either a sufficiently stout nationalism or a social order which makes independence necessary, feasible, or desirable. Some seeds of independence have been planted, however. The first shoots became visible simultaneously with a sturdier growth of the same plant elsewhere in the East after the First World War; but the soil was not propitious and the Dutch had little trouble in extirpating them. Nor is there any evidence which leads one to believe that if the Netherlands East Indies should win their freedom immediately they could long subsist as a nation. Consciousness of national identity is not yet sufficiently widespread or deeply felt. Not even the cadres of a governing class have as yet been formed. Modern ideas are disseminated very thinly. The techniques requisite to the management of a modern society have been mastered by too few. But it would be a mistake to believe that there is not discontent, that the present condition can be indefinitely projected, that the present war will not leave an ineradicable mark on the minds of the native population.

The Dutch have done much in recent years to

retrieve the unfortunate effects of rather brutal exploitation in the nineteenth century. There has been a real beginning of native representation in local government. There has been more than a beginning of managed economic development with a view to safeguarding native interests, both economic and cultural. The spirit is paternalistic, but the principle is at least one of responsible stewardship. If there must be imperialistic dominion, this is one of its better parts. Certainly it is the reverse of the unheeding exploitation that characterized nearly all such rule in the nineteenth century.

Amelioration does not seem likely to be enough, however. It is almost an unvarying rule in the relation of empires and dependencies that amelioration begets more discontent than oppression. At least the discontent becomes more intelligent and thereby more effective. Paradoxically, it can be met not by the cessation of the program of amelioration but by its accentuation. If the Dutch colonial authorities widen native participation in government in the larger centers, extend the degree of local autonomy in others, and in the more primitive centers carry out consistently the prac-

195

tice of indirect rule—administration through native leaders, to whom power is delegated but who are held responsible—then discontent can be kept within bounds. Representatives of the Netherlands government in exile have already promised that "home rule" will be introduced in the East Indies after the war and the portents for amicable relations are therefore favorable.

British Malaya is a problem of a different order. The name is a geographical convenience but a political abstraction. The area to which it is applied consists of a peninsula and outlying islands. There are the Straits Settlements, a crown colony comprising Singapore, Penang, and Malacca; the four component parts of the Federated Malay States, and the five Unfederated Malay States, so-called. All are for practical purposes British-governed, through the medium of advisers or residents. The problem of Malaya is complicated by the two factors of racial composition and natural resources. Malaya is not wholly Malay. Of a population of more than 5,000,000, the Malays are the most numerous element but still constitute a minority. They are slightly less than half the population, the rest being Chinese and Hindu, with almost three times as many of the former as of the latter.

The Malays are a people of little or no political consciousness and almost no economic capacity or interest in the modern sense of the word. They have no sense of national unity. Their only strong identification is with the individual state or locality. The only effective tie which unites them is the Moslem faith. There can be no question of giving them national independence, since there is no nation. There is only particularism in nine small localities. If Malaya were to be emancipated from British rule, the succession would not necessarily go to the Malays. It might go to the Chinese. Aside from the personnel of government, which has been British, and the small upper economic stratum, which also has been British, organized life in Malaya has been conducted by Chinese. Most commercial enterprises have been in their hands. Malaya without the Chinese would collapse economically.

The second point to be made is that Malaya is the greatest rubber and tin producing area in the world and as such is of crucial importance to the Western nations. It is one of the economic prizes

197

of the world. An area of a little more than 50,000 square miles exports normally some $300,000,000 worth of products. Since both rubber and tin are indispensable to the economy of the modern world, the normal functioning of Malaya cannot be left uncertain. The country cannot be run by Malays. It would solve no racial, ethical, or political problem to turn it over to the Chinese; indeed, Chinese rule would probably be resented more than British rule. Throughout this region there is a definite hostility to the Chinese, principally because they monopolize small business and the natives consider themselves exploited by the Chinese, sometimes justly and sometimes unjustly. It must be returned to British rule—with the qualification that a larger share of the wealth produced there should be turned back into education for the natives, that social services of all kinds should be expanded, and that the peasant and worker should be guarded against exploitation. If there is a genuine effort to teach the natives the first steps in the art of self-government and to develop them socially and economically, that is all that can be done in Malaya in the near future. Probably it is all that will be required.

There must be one common provision, however, for all the regimes established in Southeastern Asia. That has already been touched on. It is the relinquishment of trade monopolies or efforts for monopoly by the sovereign countries. Specifically, tariff restrictions must be relaxed and other restrictive measures such as quota limitations on exports abandoned. There must be free trade or a long approach thereto; or, if there are tariff duties levied for revenue or for protection of certain essential industries that could not otherwise survive against foreign competition, the tariffs must operate equally against all countries—including the country that is sovereign in the colony. In other words, Japanese goods will enter the Netherlands East Indies on the same terms as goods from Rotterdam. As has been explained, this will no doubt give Japanese goods the advantage in the Netherlands East Indies—and likewise in Indo-China and Malaya—but in the first place this is necessary in order not arbitrarily to exclude Japan from the commercial opportunities which are its by geographical situation and in the second place it is to the welfare of the native peoples. As has also been said, to deny

199

them the privilege of buying as cheaply as possible militates against their well-being, retards their development, and adds to their discontent.

In the same way no discriminations must be imposed in the outflow of strategic raw materials. Under normal peacetime conditions the question of raw materials is not so fraught with perils as is assumed in recent literature. Under normal conditions the owners of rubber plantations and tin mines and oil wells are not only willing but anxious to sell in the freest market. Except when war threatens or economic paralysis results in impediments to the free movement of exchange there are no obstacles in the way of any purchaser of raw materials. Normally there would be nothing to prevent the Japanese from buying all the rubber, oil, tin, sugar, or copra they want. Indeed, the producers would bid for their orders. In this respect, the question of apportionment of raw materials is far-fetched. International covenants binding all signatories to give unrestricted access to the natural resources under their political control are on the whole superfluous. But against pressures arising in abnormal political and economic conditions it might be advisable to covenant such guaranties. And in time, if a better mechanism of international economic operations is devised as part of the postwar system, it might be both practicable and advisable to internationalize ownership, with option on stipulated proportions of output assigned to each national group. To repeat, this is not a major issue, once the world is returned to normality. It is taken care of in the ordinary working of economic processes. The question of market, however, is vital, and it can be dealt with in such a way as to avoid friction only if there is an Open Door regime in each of the colonies. It has already been explained that such losses as accrue to the Western empires must be written off in the interests of a stable order.

What is really essential and of fundamental importance is intelligent anticipation and action accordingly. This is to say, concessions must be made to the native peoples in each of the colonies and they must be made in time. And this is to say, they must be made before they are demanded. In relations between nations, certainly in the relations between empires and dependencies, the time factor is all-important. When an action is taken is as important as what action is taken.

And with respect to concessions to subject peoples it is better to make them early or not at all; but if they are not made at all, there is no recourse except forcible repression.

Lack of foresight brought us into difficulties with the dependent peoples after 1918. It can do so again. We thought in 1918 that we could go back to 1914, both in Africa and Asia. When disaffection arose in nearly all colonial possessions, the imperial Powers could either have made concessions in placation or put down the disaffection ruthlessly and at once before it could gain force. The latter they both could not and would not do. They could not, principally because they were too spent after four years of war. They would not, because the mood to imperial grandeur had been chastened. In each of the main empires the people were disenchanted with imperial glories; there was too much cold, destructive, internal criticism, a clearer recognition of their own offenses against what can be called the law of international political decency. The people could not be whipped to any enthusiasm for distant colonial expeditions. The empires therefore did not nip rebellion in the bud; neither did they have the foresight to conciliate and thus disarm discontent by removing the cause. There were concessions later, but too late. Then they did more harm than good. Made voluntarily and before discontent has acquired momentum, concessions can win gratitude and good will and establish relations of tolerance, if not concord. Made on demand and only when demand becomes so importunate as to be dangerous, they only testify to weakness and thus invite greater demands. Success begets desire for more success, until what is asked is so egregious that collision cannot be avoided. The first rule for guidance in the relations between empires and subject peoples is this: never appease from weakness; but do appease from strength. What is given voluntarily can produce content, at least for a period. Three times as much, if given involuntarily later in order to escape the necessity of using force, will produce not content but intransigence and then the choice between fighting and surrendering. India is perhaps the best contemporary illustration. Had Great Britain in 1930 offered half of what Sir Stafford Cripps went to India in 1942 to offer . . .

The moral of this in Southeastern Asia is that

immediately after the war there must be a voluntary relaxation of foreign control in each of the colonies. Except for the Philippines and Thailand immediate emancipation is not practicable and therefore not advisable. It would settle some questions and raise others. But unmistakable evidence must be given of genuine intent to grant a greater degree of self-government. There must be increase in native participation in government, formal training of natives for administrative posts, and the opening of opportunities in the higher administrative ranks to those who have had training. The former British plan of dyarchy for India, the plan of dual control with certain powers reserved to the Crown, has in it the elements of a workable plan for the colonies in Southeastern Asia. The method, however, is less important than the principle. The native populations will recognize genuineness of intent regardless of specific measures. But intent must be present and recognizable. If in the end this means complete withdrawal, the imperial Powers will at least be able to pace the speed of withdrawal. In no circumstances can the colonies be returned to the position they occupied before. The forces of history were making that position untenable in any case, and now the war has undermined it still further. What is under way now is a process of imperial devolution. It can come at a pace determined by mutual consent, in stages agreed on and with ease of transition, or with violent wrenches. It can come peacefully or after revolts, attempts at suppression and then renewed revolts. The one thing that there cannot be is a return to the old order, and any nostalgic attempt to recall what has been will be fraught with danger and futile in the end. The only course for the West, then, is by making possible greater economic well-being and ever-increasing self-government to obtain a transitional period in which to work out a new relationship and to cushion the shock of the eventual loss.

Nothing has been said here concerning the various projects of regional federation of the colonies in Southeastern Asia which have been publicly discussed since the extension of the war to the Far East. Nothing has been said of them because they are not considered feasible—except, perhaps, as a unit in a world-wide international organization. There is too little in common among the colonies in question, too little habituation of common action or thought or interest. Any attempt to weld them into a unit would be artificial and fail as other structural devices fail when they have not a natural growth. That such projects are discussed at all testifies to the much too prevalent fallacy of dealing with political groups as if they were disembodied and inanimate. The debris of the post-1918 so-called international order is testimony to the unfortunate outcome of such fallacies.

One thing must be emphasized finally. The colonial problem in Southeastern Asia, while difficult and demanding solution, is of a lower order of importance, not comparable with the problem of adjustment of the relations between China and Japan and between both and the rest of the world. What is threatened is renewal of struggle between empires and subject peoples, which, however serious it may be and incompatible with a peacefully functioning international system, is less deadly and devastating than conflict among Great Powers for colonial prizes and imperial ascendancy.

206

Chapter Nine

Economic Deliverance Out of China

AT DIFFERENT POINTS IN THE PRECEDING PAGES the argument has been made that while the peace settlement proposed entails material losses for Western countries, the losses will be more than offset by gains otherwise arising. By any calculation exemption from war and the cost of preparation for war is ample compensation for decline in trade actual or potential, but there is something more. In addition to security, which will follow from China's emancipation and the cessation of imperialistic rivalry in the Far East, there will be more tangible returns from its strengthening through industrialization. Indeed, therein can be found one of the few signs of promise for the postwar world.

When the war is over the Western world will be in large part devastated, wholly impoverished, and confronted with the necessity of making a transition back to a peace economy. While re-building on the ruins and setting normal processes in motion, it will also have to keep people fed. On America there will fall a special responsi-bility. The prospect for this country is that of financing a gigantic world-wide W.P.A. For a few years at least we shall have to feed Europe, not because we cannot theoretically evade doing so but because practically we shall not want to evade. America cannot in its own interest permit Europe to go into dissolution either by way of slow stagnation or by way of revolution—revolu-tion not on plan or program but as mob violence and the coalescing of local disorders goaded by hunger and desperation. America cannot write off Europe politically and economically. All human considerations apart, it cannot do so. But as humanitarian considerations cannot be dismissed from consciousness, America will not want to write off Europe and will not write it off.

We shall feed Europe until crops can be sown and harvested again, and we shall give it, on credit, machinery and raw materials with which to resume production and put its people back to work. This is the only condition on which Europe can be saved from complete social regression and the only condition therefore on which we can resume economic relations with Europe. We may or may not be repaid for that which we advance; more likely not. But even if we are not repaid, it will not be total loss. We shall have our own problem of making a transition back to a peace economy, our own problem of keeping men at work when we are no longer making planes and tanks and guns. And it is better to keep them busy growing wheat and cotton and making machinery for Europe, even at taxpayers' expense, than to have 15,000,000 unemployed who also will have to be supported at taxpayers' expense. For one thing, taxes for relief will strike far harder on top of taxes to pay the war bills than they did after 1929. At least there will be some prospect that Europe can resume functioning economically and begin buying from us for cash once more. In that sense the debts owed us, though formally never repaid, will be at least partially self-liquidating, which is more than can be said of relief projects when they have to be carried out on the scale called for by so many unemployed.

The same principle will operate in the Far East,

though with a difference in degree of urgency and a still greater difference in result. For there is every prospect that we shall be repaid, with both interest and profit. It has been proposed that after the war we make China huge loans in the form of capital goods on credit—machinery and raw materials not only to rebuild what has been devastated but to establish a national industrial plant for the first time. It is through providing raw materials and machinery that we can take up the slack in production resulting from the cessation of war orders and thus cushion the shock of readjustment. And in sending technicians to help install plants and operate them until China trains its own technicians we can lessen the unemployment in the higher ranks of technical workers resulting from the closing of arms and munitions factories. As China proceeds with industrialization by means of the capital goods provided by ourselves on credit its national income will rise in equal measure and therefore its purchasing power. It will first be able to repay the loans and then buy more on direct account. For unlike Western countries China is still in the first stages of industrialization. It is as the United

States was a hundred years ago. And on all the precedents of economic history since the beginning of the machine age it can be to the United States and Europe (as well as to Japan) as the United States was to Europe in the nineteenth century—an outlet for the products of their workshops, in the last instance the employer of their workmen.

It is in the industrialization of China that there lies the best prospect for the West's recovery from the ravages of war, for the adjustment from unhealthy war prosperity to normal productive equilibrium. Still more, therein lies the best hope for the delaying of that more fundamental crisis in Western economic institutions that seemed to be growing upon us since 1918 perhaps, since 1929 certainly. For in the decades in which we are helping China to construct its modern apparatus we can find at least temporary escape from the economic impasse in which Western countries seem to have been caught. In that interval we may be able to proceed by orderly evolution toward whatever social and economic reorganization is called for—proceed by common consent and not by forcible imposition, in easy stages and not by revolutionary upheavals, by adjustment and not by expropriation. No other country than China can serve this purpose. No other country of similar size, population, and resources is still in an undeveloped stage and as ready and willing for development. Even India, for reasons peculiar to its social, racial, and political composition, does not lend itself so well. The wealth of the East, for centuries sought and mystically alluring, may be found at last—found when it is most needed, when, indeed, it can be for the West the way to economic salvation.

It is true that much lavish rhetoric has been aired in the past about the El Dorado to be found in China and that in recent years a kind of disillusionment has set in. It is therefore necessary to examine the question whether there really is any basis to the economic expectations from China or political policies have followed from nothing more than a loose boosterism. It is undeniable that the expectations have not been realized. They could not have been realized. The kind of market that China has constituted thus far, that is, a market for consumers' goods only, has limitations that cannot be transcended, in China or anywhere else. The roseate prophecies of an ever-increasing sale of goods to China because its population was enormous naturally could come to nothing as long as China was a country of peasant farming and handicraft production. Its purchasing power was limited by the volume and value of its raw materials. The elaborate calculations that China had a population of 400,000,000 and that if every Chinese bought one toothbrush and two cakes of soap and ten cigarettes and two cotton jackets every year instead of one, America would flourish, were sales promotion talk, of course. The Chinese would have been happy to buy ten times as much as they did buy abroad, but with what could they have paid? Therefore they did not. But all that has been proved thereby is that economic calculation should not be based on infectious rhetoric. Nothing has been proved with reference to China.

The commercial potentialities of any country, whether large or small, come into play only when it begins to industrialize. For only then do its demands extend beyond a narrow range of cheap commodities and only then can it pay in proportion to demand. When it is so cogently argued, as has become the fashion in recent discussion of

213

the Far Eastern problem, that the Chinese market has proved a false hope, all that is said is that China's industrialization has been delayed. The hope would have proved false in any country in which industrialism was retarded. But in a country as large as China, with as stubbornly rooted a culture as China's and suffering from as many impediments and restraints as were laid on China in the years of semisubjection, a fundamental change in the nature of society, in the structure and spirit of civilization, had to come slowly. In the circumstances the delay was not abnormally protracted. It is less than fifty years since the West moved into China in full force and the appeal of the Chinese market became a factor in political calculations, and fifty years is a short time as measured in social change. It must be remembered that although Japan is generally credited with miracles in its modernization, it was entering into the stage of effective industrialism only in the years of the First World War and to a great extent by reason of that war; and that was nearly fifty years after it had begun to industrialize. If judgment on Japan's role in world trade had been taken on the basis of 1900, thirty years after it had begun to industrialize, it could have been said, too, that Japan had no trade possibilities. In that year its imports from the whole world came to only $140,000,000. But by 1914 the total imports had increased two and a half times; by 1925 they stood at $1,250,000,-000—an increase of 900 per cent in twenty-five years. Japan had found its stride. And in recent years Japan has been America's third best customer.

Why, then, should premature conclusions be drawn with reference to China? It is considerably less than thirty years since China really began to industrialize; actually it is not much more than ten. China formally made its break with the old traditional monarchical system in 1911, and only fifteen years later was buying an average annual total of $800,000,000 worth of commodities from the rest of the world. This is as a matter of fact more than five times the amount Japan was buying from the rest of the world thirty years after it had begun to modernize and only thirty years before it had become America's best customer. The comparison is somewhat deceptive, since the total world trade was vastly larger in the 1920's

than in 1900. Yet even so the comparison is en-
lightening with respect to the disillusionment with
China's economic potentialities. China has really
just begun to industrialize. It had made notable
strides in the years before 1937, and if not ob-
structed by foreign conditions beyond its control
and, more particularly, if given the assistance
required, it will press on with increasing vigor
after the war. Only thereafter will it be possible
finally to determine how much China offers the
rest of the world by way of market. But it can be
confidently predicted that, failing obstacles arising outside itself, the curve of its foreign trade
should arise as steeply and swiftly as Japan's.
It has a larger population, a people more adapt-
able and at least as skilled as the Japanese, and
far more natural resources. Parenthetically, some
light is thrown here on the argument that no
country without an exceptionally large supply of
natural resources, among which China may perhaps be numbered, can go far in industrialization;
Japan is classic refutation. And while there is no
conclusive evidence as to China's raw material
reserves, certainly they are limitless compared to
Japan's. On all the logic of modern society and

216

by all the precedents of every other land that has
come into the system of mechanized production,
the provision of capital goods for the development
of half a continent inhabited by more than 400,-
000,000 persons should offer opportunity to the
already industrialized countries on a scale seldom
surpassed. But again it must be emphasized: only
when capital goods—machinery and plant—come
into question, not cheap commodities, consumption
goods.

With respect to this opportunity the reservation
must be stated that it will not be of unlimited
duration. In the passing of time and in direct
proportion to efficiency in modernization, China
will follow the course of other economically backward nations which have industrialized. Its plant
fully equipped, both as to production and distribution, it will cease depending on the outer world,
first for consumers' goods, then for producers'
goods, then for credit as its own surplus capital
accumulates. First it will supply its own needs,
and then, having acquired enough proficiency to
produce a surplus, it will enter into competition
for other markets with the nations which before
were its suppliers. This has been the course of

Japan; it has been the course of the United States; it will be the course of China or of any other country which newly industrializes.

The relation between the more advanced countries and an economically backward country can nearly always be described by the same curve. First there is a rise in the export of cheap consumers' goods—textiles, trinkets, simpler articles of commercial and domestic use, small tools and implements, gadgets. The rise tends to become steeper as the backward people acquire the new demands, a process that works cumulatively. Then the curve tends to flatten as the capacity to pay attains its limit; it flattens still more as the native people are tempted by the profits they see being made by the purveyance of such goods and learn to produce them themselves—textiles always in the first instance and then other commodities that can be made with less complicated tools in small shops which are essentially household industry using small power-driven implements. Then as the native people acquire greater technical proficiency and more individuals are technically trained, and at the same time there is a growing conviction among the educated classes that the nation must industrialize, the curve rises sharply again. For then new communications systems must be laid, power plants set up, roads and highways extended, mines opened, harbors dug and equipped, factories erected and machinery installed. This necessitates large purchases from abroad, and at this stage more advanced countries reap their harvest.

After that the curve flattens once more, as the newly developing country has a good enough industrial establishment to begin making its own capital goods and then to reach out for markets beyond its own boundaries, first in textiles and cheap commodities after the fashion of the countries from which it formerly bought. Then the curve may even decline, as the advanced countries are displaced first in the newly developed country itself and then in other markets to which the newly developed country is nearer and in which it has the advantage of lower costs of transportation. The decline may not be continuous, for as a nation enters fully into the industrial system it may compete at some points but its own needs increase, its trade becomes more complex, and the total value of the trade with the older countries may not diminish. In fact, as multilateral trade is extended by its own development, it may even buy more outside than it had bought before. The economic relations between England and Germany and England and the United States so appear to indicate. Whether that is true only because there were in the nineteenth century ever new regions to reach out into as England was displaced by Germany in the German market and then in more distant markets cannot be conclusively determined; there may be rigid limits to the scope of expansion for industrial societies. At any rate there is a period in which there is general leveling off of exports to newly developed countries and adjustment must be made for competition with them. It will doubtlessly be so in China too. But clearly the process is a long one, and between the time when China starts full industrialization, presumably immediately after the war, and the time when it need no longer buy capital goods from other countries but can compete with them decades must elapse, decades in which the older industrialized countries can prosper from their trade with China. Beyond that period it is not possible to calculate and it is not necessary to calculate.

220

Within that period, as was said earlier, we can make and will be compelled to make such adaptations and changes in the existing economic system as are required to keep it workable.

There may appear to be here a certain inconsistency, since in discussing the future of Japan the point was made that it would have to have economic priority in China by virtue of geographical propinquity. There is, however, neither inconsistency nor conflict. Given the development for China that is promised and the free play of economic forces, there will still be a large access of trade for Western countries even if Japan gets more than any other country or more than all others. In the first place, Japan cannot yet supply all China's needs. At that stage its own industrialization has not yet arrived, nor has it all the raw materials required. And for a few years it will be handicapped in that it will have to devote itself mainly to postwar reconstruction. This, incidentally, will serve in lieu of foreign trade to keep its workers employed, again on the premise that loans are forthcoming from the West on evidence of Japan's good behavior. In the second place, even if Japan has the larger share directly, indirectly Western countries will still be selling more to China, since Japan will have to continue to buy raw materials, semimanufactured products and machinery with which to manufacture the goods that it sells to China. From trade with China Japan will prosper. Out of the increase in demand that will follow from prosperity and the buying power yielded by prosperity more can be bought by Japan from the West. Thus not only will the West sell directly to China but indirectly through Japan as intermediary.

This is on the assumption, of course, that what we have hitherto considered economic law will not be repealed entirely by the cessation of multilateral trade. At the worst, however, even with a regime of unmixed economic nationalism operating in autarchies, the channels of international trade would still have to flow, even if the flow were controlled. Some raw materials would have to be bought in certain areas, even if they were paid for in barter. Some manufactured products could be bought more advantageously in certain countries, even if there were no international medium of exchange and payment were made in goods. Admittedly, however, the volume of trade would be seriously diminished. But if the Fascist Powers are defeated, totalitarianism unhorsed, and, what is equally important, its prestige erased, there is no reason to expect that autarchy will be the ruling principle in international economic relations. That a measure of control will have to be exercised in foreign trade is more likely than not; but even with a measure of control multilateral trade need not be abolished. The channels of trade can flow just as freely under governmental supervision as when directed by trusts, cartels, and small groups of investment bankers. Control exercised for the safeguarding of economic stability is one thing; control exercised for purposes of fortifying military dictatorship is something wholly different.

The argument that Western countries could sell more to China through Japan as intermediary was as a matter of fact skillfully pressed by Japan immediately after the invasion of China in 1937 in the hope of conciliating influential business groups in Great Britain and the United States. What difference would it make, it was said, if British and American exporters sell steel, cotton, petroleum, and finished machinery for use in

223

China to Chinese or for use in China to Japanese who govern China? Would not the effect on British and American output, British and American profits, British and American employment, be exactly the same in either case? In fact, it was argued, since the Japanese are more efficient they would build railways in China more quickly than the Chinese and thus we could sell more locomotives, repair shop equipment, steel, etc. Economically the argument was sound. To an automobile manufacturer it is immaterial whether trucks and busses used on Chinese roads are bought by Chinese for use in China or by the Japanese who control China for use in China. Under the operation of normal economic processes in accordance with traditional economic law the increment from China to all industrial countries would be the same whether China was sovereign in its own territory or Japan was sovereign in China. The flaw in the argument is that normal economic processes would not operate if Japan were sovereign. Under Japanese control China would not be developed. It would be used as a producer of primary products, its economy managed so that the benefits arising from it accrued to Japan alone. China would be abstracted from the world economy. Then indeed there would be no potentialities in China. This would be one of the first results of Japanese conquest, as it was one of the major objects of Japan's attempts to conquer.

When all the qualifications are made and the reservations entered, however, the future of an independent, reconstructed China holds high economic promise for the rest of the world. It is not necessary to theorize entirely. While admitting that China's share in world trade has not been impressive, the trend is a clear indication of potentialities already beginning to be realized. The figures are revealing. China's average annual imports between 1891 and 1900 were 180,000,000 Haikwan Taels. (The Tael was formerly the currency unit of the Chinese Maritime Customs, representing an ounce of silver and varying in value with the exchange rate for silver.) Between 1901 and 1910 the annual average was 380,-000,000 Haikwan Taels, more than double the previous decade. Between 1911 and 1915 it was 507,000,000 Haikwan Taels, one-third larger than in the previous decade—the war years are omitted as abnormal. In 1920 imports totaled

762,000,000 Haikwan Taels, another increase of 50 per cent. In 1925 they were 947,000,000 Haikwan Taels and in 1930 they were 1,309,-000,000 Haikwan Taels, an increase of more than a third in five years. In 1931 there was the Japanese invasion of Manchuria and the dislocation of both trade and statistics began. The movement upward is steady and marked. In forty years the increase was nearly tenfold. Between the beginning of the First World War and 1930 it was more than threefold. In the latter year China's purchases from the rest of the world came to nearly a billion dollars, a far from negligible figure. What is especially noteworthy is that this movement was traced before any systematic industrial development had begun. A change was just beginning to be reflected in the classification of imports. Metals and ores, metal manufactures, machinery, chemicals and automobiles and trucks were just beginning to come in. This is reflected in the fact that while in 1930-1934 machinery made up 3.5 per cent of China's imports, in 1936 it came to 6.4 per cent. In the same period metal manufactures increased from 3.5 per cent to 5 per cent, automobiles and trucks from 2.1 per cent to 5.6 per cent.

These figures are more than indicative. They are solid evidence in support of the hypothesis that can be drawn from historical and economic reasoning. China is coming into the comity of modern society. With it it brings opportunity for the rest of the world, hope of high reward, and an avenue of escape from at least some of the worst of the tribulations that lie before us in the aftermath of destruction. In building a modern China we can rebuild the more quickly on our own ruins. Economically, indeed, China is one of the few sources of hope that can now be discerned. Perhaps mainly, through it we can prolong the life of the existing economic system until we have found a remedy for its ills.

Chapter Ten

The Future for America: Good Neighbor or Empire

SOMETHING REMAINS TO BE SAID MORE SPECIFI-
cally about America's place in the Far East in
the future. Its place in the Far East in the past
has been seen, and the significance thereof can
now be apprehended. In the origin and development of America's role in that part of the world,
from occasional trading ships to plighting of its
future in the most terrible war in its history,
there is a laboratory specimen of the formation
and content of international relations in modern
times. Two hundred years ago this was a virgin
continent, inhabited by fewer than three million
persons on a thin, broken fringe along one shore.
Less than seven generations after the founding
of a republic, still on that coastal fringe and with
the whole of a continent before it, empty of people and fabulous in wealth, it finds itself in a

228

life-and-death struggle, precipitated by considerations of power and opportunities for economic gain on the other side of the globe. In other words, all the ills that the older, settled countries of Europe have long been heir to now befall America too, though the span of its history as a nation is but a moment, as history is measured in the older world. But two things should be said with reference to the fateful course America has taken in the Eastern Hemisphere. In the first place, it could not be helped, given the mainsprings of national action in modern international society. In the second place, for America as for China, the way in which the war came about conduces to the greater good in the long run or, at least, carries within itself less of evil than if it had been otherwise. Again, macabre as it may seem to find anything good in any war, nevertheless if there had to be a war at all it was better that it came about as it did.

With reference to the first: At the very end, or just before the outbreak of the war in the Far East, there entered the element of power and its obverse, security. What was clearly threatening was the formation of a gigantic Japanese empire stretching from the mid-Pacific to the Himalayas, from the Polar North to the Equator. It would be an empire containing almost a third of the population of the world and almost unsurpassed in riches. And people and riches and the power they gave would be at the disposal of a head-strong, unbridled, military autocracy, flushed with success and driven by Napoleonic ambitions for further conquest. With such an empire at full stride in the Eastern Hemisphere there would and could be no security for the rest of the world; by all the logic of international politics there would and could be no peace. Half the world would be an armed camp, ready to strike its tents and march; the other half would stand on the alert against attack. This danger alone would have been enough to warrant measures of obstruction and to lay the grounds for conflict. But before the danger had taken such proportions as to be fully perceptible and to generate commensurate fear, obstruction had already been entered by America. Indeed, as has been shown, America has stood in obstruction to Japan for a generation and has given clear indication that it would take the same position against any other country that attempted to do as Japan did. And while many motives entered, that which had most force was the economic—the insistence on an equitable share of the opportunity that lay in the development of the Far East in general, of China in particular.

The motive cannot be attributed to arbitrary willfulness, caprice, or delusion. It arises out of the ineradicable fact of social evolution in the industrial era. America, too, had arrived at industrial maturity. Having arrived, it was under the same pressure to find outlet for its surplus products as any other industrialized country. It was in a sense the prisoner of its material success, of the prodigious achievement of enhanced productivity. By habit of thought and action, in pursuance of a course laid down as early as the mid-nineteenth century, it looked to the Far East and chose China as the area of its prospective commercial expansion. And as one surveys the contemporary world, the premises being as they are, its logic is difficult to impeach. The logic has in fact been impeached by one school of historians and students of international relations, but before examining the merits of the argument it is necessary to make an observation by way of caution.

If any attempt is to be made intelligently to control the relations of nations—or of any other groups formed along any other line of division in society—it cannot be repeated too often that the soundness or fallacy of any belief is important to determine only before the belief is generally accepted and acted on. Thereafter the soundness or fallacy of the belief is irrelevant except to the historian and perhaps by way of pointing a lesson for future conduct. It is irrelevant so far as history is concerned, history in the sense of event. For if the belief is acted on, its results will be the same whether it is true or false. Thus, if Americans believed that it was necessary to have foreign trade in general and the trade of the Far East in particular, and acted as if they needed it, then the effect on Far Eastern international politics and more particularly on America's relations with the Far East was the same whether they were right or wrong in so believing. And this should have been the base from which any systematic attempt to prevent conflict in the Far East proceeded. This means that efforts should have been directed toward eliminating any possibility of clash over economic rewards in the Far

East by bringing about a regime in the Far East in which rewards could not be gained or lost by imposition of alien control and the use of imperialistic power. In other words, China would have been declared out of bounds for encroachment past encroachments would have been nullified and China would have been helped to find the means of preserving the bounds.

Now the question can be examined whether the logic of America's choice in the Far East, with all the risks that followed, is valid. Successfully to impeach the logic it is necessary to hold and to prove:

1. That an increase in exports is not necessary to the stability of the American economy.

2. That no such increase can be found in the Far East in any case.

3. Or, even if it can be found in the Far East, it can also be found in other areas, where there is less liability of political conflict.

It is not conceivable that one can seriously attempt to prove the first, to say nothing of proving that the decline that would follow from exclusion from the Far East by Japanese conquest would not be a blow seriously felt. All the most obvious

233

facts of the contemporary economy stand in evidence. American cotton, American wheat, American agricultural machinery, American automobiles, American machine products—these are not affected by expansion or contraction of the export market? England has not been affected by the decline in its textile exports? The increase in American technological efficiency since, say, 1920, has no connection with opportunity to sell more abroad—the increased output per man per hour, that is to say? The extent of unemployment will not move up or down according as we sell more or less abroad? The questions are rhetorical. They put their own answer. It is necessary only to have looked about oneself in the last ten years, to consider the policy and action of Germany in recent years, the policy and action of Great Britain, the plight of American agriculture since 1920, the curve of American employment after 1929, when Europe's purchases in this country fell off. The theory of the dispensability of exports can be held only if it is accompanied by the thesis that the necessity for exports can and should be circumvented by internal social reorganization broad enough to enable the coun-

234

try's products to be absorbed at home through redistribution of income and purchasing power. Whether or not this would suffice cannot be conclusively demonstrated in advance and need not be argued here; but until there is such a social reorganization the quest for export markets follows from a social imperative, and foreign policies that further the quest follow from a political imperative. America therefore has only been acting in obedience to the compulsions of the time.

The second proposition, that no increase in exports can be found in the Far East, was dealt with more generally in the analysis of the vindication of China's potentialities as reflected in its total trade with the rest of the world. The movement of its trade with America is still more emphatically indicative. The annual averages of American exports to China for ten-year periods are:

1891-1900	$ 8,500,000
1901-1910	24,500,000
1911-1920	37,500,000
1921-1930	103,000,000

Statistics for years following 1930 are untypical because of the war in the Far East beginning with the invasion of Manchuria.

235

What can be seen in these figures, then, is that between the last decade of the nineteenth century and the first decade of the twentieth century there was an increase of nearly 300 per cent in American exports to China; in the next ten years the increase was 50 per cent, and in the next ten years it was 178 per cent. From 1910 to 1930 American exports to China grew more than fourfold, in the thirty years from 1900 to 1930 thirteenfold. Again it must be pointed out, China's purchases in machinery and materials for industry, from which alone extensive growth can be expected, were just beginning in 1930. Something can be seen, too, in the increase in America's share in China's trade. In 1913, the last year before the European war, 7.6 per cent of China's total imports came from the United States, in 1930, 16.1 per cent—more than double—came from the United States, while Japan's share of China's imports increased by only 24 per cent and Great Britain's actually declined. America's trade with China thus was gaining faster than that of any other country. And America's share in China's total purchases increased at a higher rate than its share in the whole world's total purchases. Its share in China's purchases in the same period more than doubled; its share in the whole world's purchases increased by 18 per cent. In summary, China holds great trade potentialities for the whole world, America included. On all the evidence extant, if increase in foreign trade is essential, it can be found in China.

We come now to the third proposition, that the necessary increase in foreign trade can be found in other areas less liable to conflict than the Far East. What is usually meant is Latin America. There, it is said, lies the natural field for American enterprise. In the first place, however, Latin America and the Far East are not mutually exclusive. The United States has been striving for trade with the countries on this continent while its trade with China was going up; it has had to compete in the Far Eastern market simultaneously with its notable trade expansion in Latin America since the First World War. The one is not necessarily a substitute for the other. Trade may be necessary in both. Neither in fact can be written off. In the second place, why is it assumed that Latin America is the natural field for the economic enterprise of this country? In many respects it is more logically an outlet for Europe. Parts of it are closer to Europe than to the United States. With Europe it has a closer affinity —community of languages, community of trade practices, cultural sympathies, compatibility of traditions, and habits of association. How many countries in Latin America have a greater intellectual and spiritual allegiance to the United States than to Europe? Furthermore, Europe has economic priority in the field, at least in South America. The economy of much of South America is complementary to Europe's rather than North America's. Finally, it is doubtful whether the potentialities of Latin America are on the same scale of magnitude as China's. The population of all Latin America is not much more than a third of China's. Its people are, in large proportion, on a much lower cultural level. Therefore they can much less easily be brought within the comity of wants that industrialized societies can satisfy. Those on a lower level must undergo further cultural evolution before they can be counted for effective demand for imports from industrialized countries.

In short, then, American policy in the Far East

is an authentic product of the social environment in which the country finds itself. It is within the logic of the time—without prejudice to the question whether the time is economically out of joint or not. The motive forces of this kind of society being as they are, America has acted as it might be expected to act. The consequences are as we see them. They come by the operation of the logic of politics.

This brings us to the second point raised at the beginning of this chapter—that the war has come about in such a way as to work to the benefit of the United States in the long run in the sense that coming now and in the present circumstances it will exact a smaller sacrifice than if it had come earlier or later. To those who have followed the Far East closely it has long been clear that conflict was gathering and that it could be resolved only by war, unless some other force or event intervened to cut across the conflict. And no such force or event was perceptible; perhaps there could have been none. Increasingly the United States and Japan were drawing out as the protagonists. What appeared to be in prospect, then, even since 1918 was a war between Japan

239

and the United States over China, a war for priority in China in the old style. China would be merely a passive agent, that which was being fought for. In a war between the United States and Japan alone, with American power undistracted by the demands of another theater of war as at present, America would have to win, almost by physical law. Its superiority over Japan in man power, resources, and productive capacity turned to armament would have to be decisive in the end even if the war were prolonged by initial American reverses. Then America would be left supreme in the Far East. Its troops would be in occupation of parts of China, for the Japanese would have previously invaded at least Manchuria and North China. The American troops would have to remain at least for a period to prevent a new Japanese irruption. And if the war were long and bitter, involving heavy American losses, almost unconsciously America would assume the role of guardian over China, taking compensation in special perquisites and privileges.

America would have a claim on China's gratitude, having saved it from Japan, and it would present the claim. Not having fought in its own

240

behalf as in the present war, not yet knowing its
own power and the strength of its spirit in the
test, China would accede. Psychologically and materially, America would acquire a vested interest
in China. It would have to do so in the beginning
and then it would want to do so, because doing
so was both profitable and psychologically satisfying. Entering the Far Eastern arena in the
first instance to prevent Japanese conquest of
China, it would remain to preserve its own interest. In time it would be the object of the resentment of an increasingly nationalistic China, bent
on clearing out all intruders, the new one not
excepted. In time, too, it would be the object of
all the jealousy, suspicion, hostility of the other
Powers which it was superseding. Against it their
military and diplomatic combinations would be
directed, and against them it would form its own
combinations and aim maneuvers in turn. America
would find itself in the classic imperialistic position, with all the hostages that are given when
that position is taken—the principal hostage being
sure commitment to war.

All this is spared America now. Now, for
reasons already explained, China is not passive.

It is not being saved by America; it has saved itself. America will have no vested interests and will not be able to remain in China to preserve them. It will have no primacy in China to generate fear and resentment on the part of other Powers. The war will not be just one campaign in a war to be resumed later, with China still the prize of victory. The postponement of the war until China had found itself has prevented all that. Therefore, coming now rather than earlier, the war will entail less human suffering for America, a smaller sacrifice of blood and treasure.

It will also entail less suffering than if it had come later—that is, after a Japanese victory in China or a stalemate, with Japan remaining in occupation of large parts of China. For this would be postponement of a larger war rather than prevention. The very accretion of power to Japan would stir American apprehension. America would be excluded from trade with any part of the Far East, especially with China. It would have access to the tin and rubber of Malaya and the Netherlands East Indies on Japan's sufferance and subject to Japanese blackmail. For an interval America might submit, depending in part on the result of the European conflict. But in light of all that America has stood for in the Far East and, still further, in light of the fact that the pressure for foreign trade would increase rather than diminish after the years of war in both Asia and Europe, it is inconceivable that American submission would be for more than an interval. And in that interval it would call on all its resources materially, morally, technically. Naval and aerial construction would go forward at a frantic pace, and for the first time in American history there would be a huge standing army commensurate with the size of the population, and armament in proportion. Japan would become apprehensive and arm equally feverishly. The conventional armament race would set in. Each side would maneuver for position and for allies. The clash would come. In all probability it would come in circumstances more unfavorable than at present. Japan would then have the resources of all Eastern Asia at its disposal. China would not be an ally as at present, for after a long period of subjection to Japan it would not have the means to act even if its spirit were not broken. The war would be long and deadly. And if America were victorious, it would come out of the war a great military power, its objects and ambitions quite likely transmuted by military success. Then, too, China would be politically inanimate. Japan's Asiatic empire would disintegrate in defeat, and since politics, too, abhors a vacuum America would be the inheritor. In a sense it would not be able to help itself, and, besides, it would not want to help itself. Its sacrifices would make compensation seem just, and power begets desire for more power. Then, too, America would enter on the path of empire.

Seen in perspective, what is being fought out now on the battlefields of Europe, Asia, Africa, and the Pacific Islands is America's place in the world in the future. Apart from the question of national survival, this is for America the most important issue raised by the war. Is America to continue on its traditional course as laid down in the beginning or is it to embark on a new course— that of conquering or at least contending empire? Is it to set forth on a great career of imperialistic conquest, in spite of itself, perhaps even against its will? Paradoxically, the danger of the latter has been diminished by America's entry into the

World War rather than increased. Paradoxically, too, the danger lies not so much in victory as in defeat; not by victory but by defeat will the impetus to conquer be given.

In victory the United States will still have some option as to the kind of role it would play in the world—with the reservation that has been made for the Far East. There victory will not confer any opportunity for extension of political influence, since China too will be victorious and at least in the first postwar stages unchallengeable in its own territory. In Europe too there will be some restriction on America's freedom of choice, for in victory Great Britain will emerge intact, France will be reconstituted, and Russia will be a factor to be reckoned with. America will have tremendous economic power but will not be able to translate that into political power, so long as there are great states jealous of their position and prerogatives. Therefore, parenthetically, much of the contemporary talk about America's assumption of world leadership after the war (if the war is won by the United Nations) can be dismissed as rhetoric—overheated and politically naïve rhetoric if it sounds the theme of so-called American centuries, sentimental and politically naïve rhetoric if it sounds the theme of international virtue under American tutelage. Europe has never been in a mood to abdicate to America; it will be furthest from such a mood if it escapes subjection to Germany. Furthermore, however much Europe respects America's industrial might and potential military prowess, it has never modified its conviction that America is politically adolescent. The last is almost the only conviction on which all Europe is united. America's freedom of choice will be restricted in Europe in the sense that a limit will be put upon any potential American hope to exercise power of decision, but this will be a restriction that inures to America's welfare in the long run. Any unrestrained exercise of authority over Europe would before long generate as much hostility in Europe toward America as there had previously been within Europe. In Latin America, however, the United States will have full option as to its role if victorious.

In defeat, however, America would have little or no option. The choice would be forced; it would have to aspire to conquest as a means to security. And it would do so. There is no contradiction between this and defeat. A country as large, rich, and powerful as America cannot be permanently crushed or even for long subdued. It could not be devastated. Recuperative powers would be generated from within and in a few years it would have recovered. There would thus be a lull in which breath was regained and wealth and energy replenished. Then measures would be taken to avoid repetition of defeat. America would seek to make itself impregnable in the traditional way—anticipating encroachments by making them. It would have to do so. The choice would lie between doing so and submitting permanently to obscurity, a submission no people will make unless negligible in strength and subdued in spirit, as this country is not and need not be. There are three regions in which the United States would proceed to fortify itself by advance as a measure of defense: The Far East, Canada, and Latin America.

What can be foreseen in the Far East has already been discussed. The urgency would be more immediate in Canada and Latin America. It can be taken for granted that unless the United States were permanently and irredeemably impotent, it would not remain inert while a new military

Power consolidated itself in Canada. As soon as it recovered poise it would begin pushing influence into Canada, at first economically and then politically, relying on penetration after the manner of the nineteenth century rather than open aggression. Sooner or later it would give the challenge for supremacy in the former Dominion, having the advantage of propinquity. It would do so first with the sympathy and support of Canadians seeking to throw off the European thrall. If the effort were successful a new set of complications would enter. Canada, though emancipated and sovereign in its own right, would have to depend on the United States for protection. Still more would it have to depend on the United States for capital both to underwrite its industries and to develop the still untapped resources.

This would not be altogether new. To a certain degree Canada has been an economic tributary of the United States in the past. The investments of the United States in the Dominion have been second only to Great Britain's. Through ownership of branch factories, through investments, and as the principal purchaser of some of Canada's products, the United States has had at

248

least potential economic power in the Dominion. So long as Canada's political status remains beyond question, which is to say so long as it is a part of the British Commonwealth and has behind it the power of the British Empire, the relation of economic tributary to the United States raises no serious problem. British political and military power precludes any of the considerations that arise as between, say, the United States and Cuba. But if the British Empire were crushed and Canada were ostensibly on its own but actually dependent on America, a new order of relations would be established. First we would extend protection to Canada with its consent. It would have no choice. Then it would be irked at having to do so. As is generally known, Canada is sensitive with regard to the United States, partly because at times the United States has not been overdelicate in word and act. There would be resentment on Canada's part, for the relation of tributary would no longer be moderated or counterbalanced by British power. There would be reluctance on the part of the United States to make remission of rights and privileges. The traditional psychological sequence in the relations of the strong and weak would set in. As between the United States and Canada it would be as it was in the past between the United States and Latin America—overweening power on one side; fear, suspicion, resentment on the other. And power, challenged, would have to assert itself.

In Latin America, however, the real test would come. A German or Japanese invasion of Latin America and the formal planting of German and Japanese colonies would be unlikely; they would also be unnecessary. There would be other ways of accomplishing German and Japanese purposes, which would be, of course, the exercise of effective hegemony and the acquisition of positions from which to menace or at least blackmail the United States. Occasions would offer themselves. Suppose, for example, that sometime after the consummation of a German-Japanese victory there were an election in, say, Panama. Mr. A, the defeated candidate, having started to plot against his successful rival and being detected, would flee to Cuba, say, for safety. There he would be approached by emissaries of the German consulate, who would commiserate him on the injustice done him and inquire solicitously whether anything could not be done to restore justice. Mr. A. would be receptive. Soon there would be established in Panama a dyestuff importing agency, say, with an open credit of half a million marks. Out of this sum German friends in Panama of Mr. A's German friends in Cuba would begin buying the good will of dissident Panamanian military men and politicians. They would also buy machine guns, rifles, and grenades and with the connivance of willing or purchasable customs officers slip them across the frontier as dyestuffs— the familiar practice of insurrecto gun-running. Then there would be a revolution. The president would be driven out; Mr. A would assume the presidency. In simple gratitude he would then give his German friends a concession to operate two airlines, one going south to South America and the other north to Mexico—incidentally, flying over the Panama Canal.

The United States would see the point. The evicted president meanwhile would have taken refuge in Miami. There American gentlemen would approach him. After some preliminary conversations the American gentlemen would start an automobile agency in Panama with an open credit of a million dollars. They, too, would win over with discreet expenditures generals, politicians, and customs inspectors. They, too, would slip in as automobile parts machine guns, rifles, and grenades. There would be another revolution. Mr. A would be out. The evicted president would return. The airline concessions to the German friends would be canceled. And this time the Americans would see to it that the president stayed and Mr. A was kept out. And if and when the partisans of Mr. A or others of similar inclinations began plotting, Americans would supply the incumbent government with guns and money and, if that were not sufficient, would send the U. S. Marines. So much strength America would soon have, especially as it could get there sooner than Germany or Japan.

Then would we wait until Germans had fomented revolutions in Nicaragua, Venezuela, Peru, and other countries, installed puppet regimes, and obtained air bases near the Panama Canal and within striking distance of Houston, New Orleans, Birmingham? Would we wait until puppet regimes were set up and then have to overthrow them? We would not. We would take preventive measures. We would see to it that in each republic there was a government sympathetic to ourselves, perhaps compliant with our wishes and, if necessary, subject to our veto. Where these conditions were met in the natural course of local politics, there would be no occasion for extraordinary complications. But as politics go in the less secure republics, circumstances would almost certainly arise in which it would be necessary to exert supervision and probably, in time, to install governments of our own choosing.

The result, even without German instigation, would inevitably be a resurgence of suspicion of Yankee imperialism, a thorough disillusionment with the short-lived Good Neighbor policy as having been hypocritically adopted for political purposes, and a return of the old bitterness at the Colossus of the North. There would be anti-United States parties. Opposition to the United States would be capitalized for internal party purposes and popular antagonism to the United States exploited. In time there would be anti-United States coups. Then we should be back where we were between 1900 and 1928, with intervention by the Marines to put down risings or chronic

253

disturbance, and then full occupation to prevent further risings. The Colossus of the North would be feared, resented, and hated again. Those who have traditionally distrusted the pushful Yankee would find vindication of their warnings that the Yankee devil had wanted to be a monk only when he was sick.

The point is this: *for the United States there would be nothing else to do.* We might deplore, we might hate, what we were doing, and we might be able to foresee the ugly consequences; but we would have no alternative. No anti-imperialist, however devoted to his cause and intellectually convinced of its soundness, would be able to make an effective case for any other course.

What would happen if America just did nothing? What would prevent the Germans from backing one side in internal political feuds in one or more Latin-American republics, laying the successful party under obligation, and taking compensation in economic, political, even military concessions? What would prevent the Japanese from undertaking economic penetration, then intervening to support their vested interests, and then continuing to control through the medium of a puppet regime? Or what would prevent them from fomenting internal dissension and civil wars, so that they would have a pretext for intervening?

All this is not unprecedented. It is not unique to Fascism or Germans or Japanese. It is orthodox procedure in small weak countries in which Great Powers have interests or strategic designs. It has been practised in various places in Africa and Asia. Japan has made effective use of it in China in the past. The result in Latin America would be to establish at our doors a kind of Balkan tinderbox which could be used by Germany and Japan just as the Great Powers have used the European prototype. In other words, each controlled republic would be used as a pawn, as an entering wedge, as a cloak for larger purposes. Each would become a moving outpost advancing toward the United States as a threat.

In elementary considerations of security we could not remain inert. Only an American of other-worldly innocence or irredeemable stupidity about politics would advocate sitting inert while European and Asiatic empires were planting outposts within gunshot. Applying the Monroe Doctrine would not be just a matter of tradition but

255

a matter of survival, and if and when America had the strength once more it would fight. It would have to fight. But it would first attempt obstruction without fighting. The Monroe Doctrine in its negative function, as the levying of injunctions, would not be enough as obstruction. A more positive interpretation would have to be given. Before Germans or Japanese could go so far as to establish outposts on this continent, the United States would seek to eradicate their influence. It would first counter every German or Japanese coup, maneuvered directly or through native pawns, by overthrowing the puppet regimes set up by the coups. And it would, unofficially but effectively, visa other governments in Latin America only if warranted to be immune from use as German or Japanese pawns. To be on the safe side it would have to exercise a certain degree of supervision. This would be a matter of self-defense—of the offensive that is the best defense. And there would be no alternative. But therein would lie one of the poignant tragedies in the history of the New World. For it would decree the death of the Good Neighbor policy.

The Good Neighbor policy has been more than

diplomatic policy. It has carried emotional freight. It has had almost spiritual significance in the relations between the two halves of the American continent. A pause has been given to what had appeared to be the glacial imperialism of the United States, a kind of slow but remorseless southward movement of domination.

From the middle of the 1890's to the Hoover administration there were all the stigmata of the classical relation of aspirant empire and prospective dependency. Then, beginning with Hoover and carried forward under Roosevelt and Hull, there was a reversal; measured against the political forces of the time, it was an astonishing reversal. An apparently irresistible trend had been halted; a trend in the opposite direction had set in. There was an effort for psychological reconciliation as well as political reconciliation. Indisputably there has been—and almost for the first time—the beginning of mutual trust between the United States and the countries to the south of it. For the first time in decades there has been a belief in Latin-American countries that the United States, though powerful, could be trusted.

257

For the first time, incidentally, the United States has moderated its air of insolent patronage.

There has been no political event on this continent more significant than that of Mexico's expropriation of American-owned oil wells and the sequel. This has no parallel in modern times in the relations between strong nations and weak nations. Against the background of all the historical friction between the two countries, Mexico, a poor and weak country, confiscated property worth millions of dollars belonging to the citizens of an omnipotent neighboring country, citizens belonging to the most influential groups in that country. And the omnipotent country, in which less provocation had often in the past brought demands for intervention, not only did not intervene, but took no reprisal. It patiently negotiated and accepted settlement on terms constituting defeat for itself. It is difficult, if not impossible, to find a comparable instance of abstention from the use of power, by a state which had the power, in a situation in which there was so much at stake. The significance of that has not been lost on the rest of Latin America.

The comparison with what took place in the

years of Theodore Roosevelt, Taft, Wilson, Harding, and Coolidge makes the words Good Neighbor something more than a rhetorical conceit. It signifies a genuine change of attitude. A basis has been laid for mutual trust and understanding, for co-operative action on this continent, for the first time since James Monroe and John Quincy Adams. A century of unfortunate history is apparently being undone. For the first time there has appeared to be substantial ground for concord among the Americas, though the close juxtaposition of weak and strong nations has almost always been an unfavorable portent for political harmony. This beginning, if not cut short, may one day count as one of the significant historical developments of this period. Its end would be one of the tragic consequences of the Second World War—tragic because inescapable if the war were won by Germany and Japan.

In Latin America, in Canada, in the Far East it would be the same. In spite of itself, perhaps against its will, but to save itself, America would have to strive for power. And thus it would be chained to the wheel of endless warfare, that which it hoped to escape in its founding. If it succeeded, it would wield power. Wielding power, it would be compelled to defend it and would want to defend it. It would be engaged in the imperial struggle, no longer negatively, no longer preventively, no longer just seeking to lay injunctions against others, but in preservation of its possessions, perquisites, and prestige. It would be as other empires—enjoying for a season the refulgence of imperial glory and then paying the terrible reckoning, as witness the history of Europe in the last forty years. Whether this shall be, whether it must be—for America that is perhaps the highest stake of the war. If the United Nations win, it need not be; it is indeed less likely to be now than if America had kept out of the war and the Fascist Powers had won. Therefore, if there had to be a war at all, if America had to be drawn into war at all, it is not an unmixed evil that it was drawn in now. Viewed in the long perspective it was not wholly unfortunate that the Far Eastern war came as it did and thereby plunged America into the world maelstrom.

Epilogue

ONE WORLD IN THE FAR EAST HAS GONE DOWN in war; it could not do otherwise. Now it is for us to determine what shall succeed: a world in which peace can subsist or one in which the forces that march to war are set in motion again, as at Versailles in 1919. If we have foresight and the wisdom to draw the lesson of the past, we can have the former. It is neither impossible nor, by comparison with Europe, difficult to lay the basis for a lasting peace in the Far East. To do so we must:

Crush Japan, drive it out of the Asiatic continent, and then give it a just, even generous peace. Give it the possibility to live and prosper, even help it toward attaining a fuller material life if there is evidence of abandonment of the old militarist ambitions.

Liberate China, make it independent in law and fact. Voluntarily withdraw from it politically ourselves as completely as we forcibly eject Japan. Give it assistance toward making itself strong enough to repel all future aggression and toward reconstruction by industrialization.

Set in motion at once the process of introducing self-government in the colonies of Southeastern Asia. By education and opportunity to gain experience prepare the inhabitants to take over the control of their own affairs, and as they give evidence of capacity for self-government begin the process of withdrawal. Meanwhile institute a regime of free trade in the colonies or at least of most-favored-nation treatment for all countries, the imperial sovereign included, with tariffs only for revenue required to meet costs of administration.

Renounce all gains won in the past and gains of the same kind expected in the future—the preferred political positions we had, the economic monopolies we hoped to keep or expected to get. This means undoing the past, uprooting the whole imperialistic system of a hundred years. But in compensation therefor there will be the returns that lie in the free economic development of the Far East, of China in particular. Still more, there

will be the compensation that lies in extricating
the Far East from the war system and absolving
ourselves from the periodic sacrifice of blood and
treasure that will be exacted by that system if it
becomes as deeply rooted in the Far East as it is
in Europe. This alone is enough to counterbalance
any loss voluntarily written off, whether economic, material, or psychological. To get it no
price is too big. For without it we shall not survive
as economies, as states, as a civilization; instead,
socially and biologically the life blood will be
drained out of us by the kind of chronic political
hemophilia that is emaciating Europe.

INDEX

Adams, John Quincy, and Latin America, 259
Air power, destruction of Japanese cities by, 72-73
America; *see* United States
America, Latin; *see* Latin America
Appeasement in Southeastern Asia, 201-205
Asia; *see* China, Far East, Japan, Southeastern Asia
"Asia for the Asiatics," 181; *see also* New Order
Australia, Japanese islands divided between America and, 68-69
Authoritarianism in Japan, 76, 149; *see also* Feudalism
Authority, constituted, versus individual rights, 88-89
Autonomy in Far East for lasting peace, 57
Axis; *see* Germany, Japan

Birth control in China, need for, 112
Bolsheviks, 121
Britain; *see* Great Britain
British Malaya
  Japan's economic priority in, 160
  after Second World War, 196-198

Burma after Second World War, 183-185

Canada and United States, relations between, 247-250
Canute, 168-169
Capital goods, American, for China, 210
Chiang Kai-shek, 102
China; *see also* Far East
  aggression by, improbable, 128-134
  agrarian reforms needed in, 116
  American guardianship of, undesirable, 240-241
  American interest in, evolution of, 29-34
  American intervention in, during nineteenth century, 49-50
  American loans to, after war, 210-211
  American sympathy for, 32
  American trade with, 37-54, 235-238
  as America's area of commercial expansion, 231-232
  America's backing of, against Japan, 52-54
  capital needed for reconstruction of, 108, 110, 210

265

INDEX

266

INDEX

China—*Continued*
revolution in, possible future, 120
rivalry over, 93-94; *see also* Great Powers
Russia's future relations to, 120-128
trade with, beginnings and growth of, 37-54, 225-227
unification of, 104-118; *see also* China, reconstruction of
victory by, Western Powers' position in the event of, 61-63
war inevitable for, 100-101
Chinese-American t r e a t y of 1842, 40-42
Chinese Nationalist Party, 24
Civilization
definition of, 87
European, composition of, 87-88
Germany and Japan outside comity of their, 89
Japanese, evolution of, 74-90
Clan organization, 114, 147
Cleveland, Grover, and annexation of Hawaii, 47
Colonial revolts, nationalism as cause of, 21-22, 23
Colossus of the North, 253-254
Communism
in China, 24-25, 118-119, 126-128
in Indo-China, 191
world-wide, 121-122
Communist International; *see also* Russia
in Southeastern Asia after First World War, 180

Confucianism, 82
Coolidge, Calvin, and Latin America, 258-259
Cripps, Sir Stafford, in India, 203
Cuba in war with Spain, 47-48
Cushing, Caleb, 40

Daimyo, 77-78
Dictatorship in Germany, inevitability of, 89-90
Diet, the Japanese, 80
Dutch East Indies, Japan's economic priority in, 160, 194-196

East, the; *see* Far East, Southeastern Asia
East Indies; *see* Dutch East Indies
Economic law, 222-224
Emperor worship in Japan, 76-80
England; *see* Great Britain
Equality of opportunity in China, 49-54
Europe
America's feeding of, after Second World War, 208-209
America's isolation toward, 30-31
attitude of, toward America, 246
and the Far East
contrast between, as to peace problems, 5-8
wars of, joined, 26
and Latin America, trade between, 237-238
politics of, 6-7, 31

267

INDEX

Feudalism
  in Europe, Church's influence
    on, 85
  in Japan
    evolution of, 76-85
    persistence of, 144-147
Fillmore, Millard, and Amer-
    ica's role in the Pacific,
    39-40, 42
First World War
  colonial dependencies after,
    177-178
  Germany after, mistake con-
    cerning, 91-92, 131
  and imperialism in Southern
    Asia, 178-179
  prelude to, 15-18
  and Second World War, com-
    parisons between, 1-2
  and Southeastern Asia, 178-
    180
Formosa, return of to China, 68
France
  China's partitioning planned
    by, 49
  Colonial policy of, 193
  fall of, factors in, 130-131
  in First World War and
    Southern Asia, 179
  in Hawaii, interest of, 38
  and Indo-China, relations be-
    tween, 190-192
  and Japan, agreement be-
    tween, 10-11
  Japan's contempt for, 192
  after Second World War, 245
  and Thailand, 188-189
French Indo-China; *see also*
    Indo-China
  Japan's economic priority in,
    160

Germany
  China's partitioning planned
    by, 49
  crushing of, essential, 91-92
  export policy of, 234
  after First World War, 73,
    131
  and Great Britain, economic
    relations between, 220
  and Japan, similarities be-
    tween, 85-92
  military caste in, 91
  recovery of, after First World
    War, 73
  victory by, effects of, 250-256
  war attitudes unchanged in,
    89
Good Neighbor policy, 256-259;
    see also Latin America
Great Britain; *see also* Great
    Powers, Western Powers
  China's partitioning planned
    by, 49
  China's settlement with, after
    Second World War, 97
  colonial policy of, social arro-
    gance in, 191
  in European wars, role of, 5
  export policy of, 234
  in First World War, and
    Southeastern Asia, 179
  and Germany, economic rela-
    tions between, 220
  in Hawaii, interests of, 37-38
  imperialism of, in China, 24
  and India, 185, 203-204; *see
    also* India
  and Malaya, 198
  after Second World War,
    245; *see also* Peace

269

INDEX

270

INDEX

INDEX

272

INDEX

Oil
  Mexico's expropriation of American, 258
  sale of, to Japan, 13
Open Door policy
  beginnings of, 40-41
  China's, 160-163
  and Great Powers, in Chinca, 49-51
  in Southeastern Asia, 199-201
Orient; *see* Far East, Southeastern Asia
Osaka, 146

Pacific, war in the; *see also* Far East, war in, Second World War
  prelude to, 10-28
Peace
  economic forces in Far East involved in, 160-168
  economy, return to, difficulties involved in, 208-209
  in the Far East, basis for, 4-8, 55-64, 97-98, 261-263; *see also* Great Powers
Pearl Harbor, 1, 2, 9, 10, 13, 20, 54
Penang, 196
Perry, Commodore, 42-43
Philippines; *see also* Southeastern Asia
  American occupation of, reasons for, 47-49
  Japan's economic priority in, 160
  after Second World War, 185-188
Population problems
  in China, 111-113

Population Problems—*Cont.*
  in Japan, 138-139, 141-142, 166-167, 171-172
Power Politics, 129-130
Powers; *see* Great Powers, Western Powers

Railroad, transcontinental, influence of Far East on, 43-44
Raj, 184
Reconstruction, 107; *see also* China, reconstruction of, Japan, reconstruction of
Restoration, the, in Japan, 76, 80
Roosevelt, Franklin D., and Good Neighbor policy, 257-258
Roosevelt, Theodore, 32, 37, 258-259
Rubber, 242
  in Malaya, 197-198
Russia; *see also* Communism
  and America, relations between, after Second World War, 124-125
  in China, intervention of, 23-25
  China's integrity threatened by, 51-53
  China's partitioning planned by, 49
  dependence upon Great Britain and United States, 123
  and Far East, future relations between, 120-128
  and Japan, war between, 17, 51-53

274

INDEX

INDEX

276